Eye of the Storm

Inside City Hall During Katrina

Sally Forman

by

Sally Forman

authorHOUSE®

AuthorHouse™
1663 Liberty Drive, Suite 200
Bloomington, IN 47403
www.authorhouse.com
Phone: 1-800-839-8640

First published by AuthorHouse 8/20/2007

ISBN: 978-1-4343-2997-4 (sc)
ISBN: 978-1-4343-2998-1 (hc)

Library of Congress Control Number: 2007905854

Printed in the United States of America
Bloomington, Indiana

This book is printed on acid-free paper.

For the heroes who so bravely rescued our citizens including all city, state, federal and international military, law enforcement, fire and emergency personnel.

Chaplains' prayer for bodies discovered after Katrina:

We give thanks that this person was found.
We give thanks for the persons that found them.
We ask that they may be made whole in God's arms
and that they know peace.

Contents

Introduction

Right Smack in the Mirror

"This is important," I said to Mayor Ray Nagin while crossing through the formal seating area in his second floor office at City Hall. "Were you ever – I mean *ever* – a Republican?" Sitting across the expansive mayoral desk, I looked at him intently.

"Never, ever," he laughed. "Why?"

"Because that's the latest rumor flying across the country right now."

"Any legs to it?" he asked.

"Unfortunately, yes."

Rumors had been circulating almost every day since Hurricane Katrina struck – tall tales such as a third of our Police Department was phantom officers, or the Mayor had moved to a fancy home in Dallas, and even one that our drinking water would kill unsuspecting citizens within two days of consumption. While many of the flagrant lies faded quickly, several took root, requiring me to work rapidly to kill the chatter before reputable sources grabbed hold of it.

I provided the Mayor only the most pertinent information. "It's been reported you were a Republican until just a few days before you ran for Mayor in 2002," I said. "*The Washington Post* ran with it and now it's posted on Wikipedia."

"That's interesting," he said.

"I'll call the *Post* on my way home," I informed him.

It was October 2005. Since evacuating after Katrina, my family had moved to Baton Rouge. Just two months earlier, I had lived 15 minutes from my job at City Hall, my teenage children attended neighborhood schools and my beloved New Orleans was the soul of America, a rich, cultural treasure with over 70 distinct neighborhoods. Now I commuted four hours a day as family and friends lay scattered and our city remained a dormant ruin.

As I drove home that evening, my tense shoulders and arms finally relaxed on the wheel. I drifted into thought and began to contemplate the pros and cons of writing a book about what happened in the city during the storm. A project this large would most likely require me to resign my job as communications director for Mayor Nagin and the City of New Orleans so I had to share these prevailing thoughts with the Mayor.

"We need to tell the real story of what took place during the storm and in the aftermath so that history is recorded," I finally said to him one day. "More importantly, this will help other cities be more prepared for catastrophes."

The Mayor sat up straight in his black leather chair, weighing his response with one eyebrow raised. "There's too much work for you to do right now," he said. "And besides, I don't want your first book to be on this."

I didn't like what he said but was too busy for a battle, as my workload had shot up tenfold since the storm.

Then in January 2006, another storm hit on Martin Luther King Jr. Day, when Mayor Nagin gave a speech now famous for its racially and politically divisive words. Never pulling his prepared text out of his pocket, the Mayor challenged the African American community to fix itself. "We're not taking care of our children when you have a community where 70 percent of its children are being born to one parent," he said.

He closed his remarks, however, by stating that God was now sending hurricanes because He was mad at America and that New Orleans would be a majority black population, describing it as a "chocolate city," because God would want it that way.

With this one senseless speech, Ray Nagin touched off a firestorm that drove a bevy of 22 opponents seeking to unseat him as Mayor. I remain convinced that without that speech, his opposition would have been nominal.

Oddly, one of those who stepped up to unseat him was Ron Forman, my husband. Although I didn't understand fully his intentions at the time, Ron's simple goal was to right the ship by offering a different style of leadership to the city. Reluctantly, I abruptly resigned from my government post to stand by my husband.

Katrina was the worst natural disaster in the history of our country, devastating a section of America equal to the size of England. As our city struggled for air, I trusted we would learn from our mistakes. Our response to a storm that had been predicted for years showed we still had a lot of work to do in disaster management throughout all levels of government. And it was clear the first place to identify these breakdowns was right smack in the mirror.

In New Orleans, a city that sits below sea level, hurricane experts warned for years about the effects of "the big one." Still, citizens had fallen into a mode of complacency since a major storm had not hit the city since Hurricane Betsy in 1965. Knowing this mindset existed, city leaders for decades relied on emergency planning methods that did little to alter this public outlook. Also, plans that existed in our emergency preparedness guidelines, including arrangements to evacuate poorer citizens, were not as well rehearsed as they could or should have been, resulting in some key personnel possessing only a basic awareness of the city's command and control structure.

On the state level, the challenges proved equally as chaotic, but state officials had the benefit of viable communications during and after the storm. The state was charged with sending resources into the city, but safety concerns caused much help to be turned away. While a vulnerable population was in need of rescue, bureaucratic rules that stalled progress could and should have been discarded faster than a smelly refrigerator. Topping it off, some state officials allowed politics to influence critical stages of the response.

On the federal level, the lack of operational command in the Department of Homeland Security left a gaping hole in the disaster response, despite the fact that supplies such as water and MRE's (meals ready to eat) were in place before the storm. After our levee system failed, no observable operational structure to manage the incident and coordinate local, state and federal level support kicked in, and no federal official emerged immediately as a leader. For the first several days, the White House seemed at best reactive, and at worst clueless, about what was actually taking place in the city.

Shortly after the storm, the U.S. Congress created the House Select Bipartisan Committee to Investigate the Preparation for and Response to Hurricane Katrina. A Senate panel led by Republican Senator Susan Collins and then-Democratic Senator Joe Lieberman assembled a similar investigative panel. But much of what had happened on the inside, beyond the eyes and ears of the nation, would remain untold.

I mulled over a number of issues before deciding to write this story. Was it necessary to share the information that I had, I asked myself, knowing unknown stories might hurt good, well-intentioned people? Maybe if I waited long enough, I hoped, the adverse effects would diminish. Did I really want to wander back into the days after the storm, knowing I would again smell the stench and feel the anguish that occurred? Only if this could help another city in a crisis, I decided. But would people understand that this was simply one person's point of view on the events as they unfolded during that time? Depending on each individual's perspective, I imagined several different conclusions could be drawn from almost every significant detail about the hurricane. But this is my story and, based upon what I personally observed, these are my own conclusions.

Katrina was an anticipated natural disaster, but government at every level still failed. I was part of that government. With terrorist attacks and natural disasters a continued threat, my hope is that this portrait of a city in crisis can help prevent similar problems when the next disaster strikes.

Prologue

Pass the Smelling Salts

Thursday, August 25

I rolled out of bed Thursday morning, slipped on my beloved pair of fuzzy pink slippers, checked my Blackberry and walked outside to get the newspaper. As I stepped on the sidewalk, our three-year-old spaniel, an adorable white cocker that had been abandoned in a grocery cart at a Home Depot, was scratching the window barking at me. We named the dog Barq's after a local root beer and, for the amount of yelping he did, the name suited him perfectly.

I scanned the headlines as I walked back into the house, noting no stories of concern. As I drank a soothing cup of café au lait, I fed Barq's, got myself and my kids ready, took my vitamins, kissed my husband goodbye and jumped in the SUV to tackle carpool and another day of work.

My job as communications director for the City of New Orleans and Mayor C. Ray Nagin was always bustling with key messages to convey to the public, numerous calls and e-mails to return, staff issues to manage and small emergencies to triage.

The Communications Department consisted of six offices for which I was responsible: Special Events, Community Affairs, Press, Production, Special Projects and Design. Each department was small, but our mission was clear: effectively communicate critical public information and the Mayor's vision of social and economic revitalization to the citizens of New Orleans. After creating a theme entitled "One New Orleans," we launched a television show and magazine under that brand.

Scheduling the Mayor was another one of my key priorities, ensuring that he spent equal amounts of time with business, the community and civic groups. Whether it was visiting dignitaries, public officials or community leaders, somebody was always requesting official attention. "Engelbert Humperdinck is in town," wrote a V.P. from Universal Music that day, asking for an official welcome to New Orleans.

People loved coming to New Orleans. The Cajun and Creole food, the jazz and soul music playing on our streets and in our clubs, and the majestic Spanish and French architecture that lined our streets brought over 10 million tourists a year. David Letterman said it best while broadcasting from our city one night: "This is the most interesting damn city in America."

Visitors included conventioneers, families of tourists, party animals and, increasingly, movie stars, since attractive state tax incentives for filmmaking had turned New Orleans into "Hollywood South." But like a Hollywood set, New Orleans had a majestic exterior with a hollow interior.

Almost all of the public schools had been failing for generations, leaving the city's poorest people functionally illiterate, without opportunity, and pushed all too often toward a life of crime. "New Orleans is a dying city, and one of the reasons it is dying is because of the educational system," former Louisiana Senate President John Hainkel once railed while noting that three generations had now cycled through a broken and mismanaged system.

In addition, the city's murder rate was climbing to one of the highest in the country with only Camden, New Jersey, showing a higher per capita rate in 2004. Distrust between the community and the Police Department was rampant. Bankrupt of civility, some neighborhoods in New Orleans had become more dangerous than Baghdad.

This state of affairs left government officials the complicated task of tirelessly offering hope to a citizenry that was, in many respects, hopeless.

Our schedule on August 25 began with a public appearance at a statewide litter conference. "The streets of New Orleans should be as clean as Disney," the Mayor said in his speech, careful not to place the word "buildings" in the same sentence as Disney, a taboo for staunch preservationists living in the city.

Our second stop was the U.S. Mint in the French Quarter for a cultural summit hosted by the personable Lieutenant Governor Mitch Landrieu. In his second address of the morning, the Mayor said, "We will create economic growth by supporting the 'trinity industries' of music, film and digital media," reminding me of the holy trinity of food in New Orleans-onion, bell pepper and celery-every time he said it.

After the summit, we left the French Quarter and drove downtown to local television station WDSU to tape our monthly TV show. I arrived before the Mayor and scanned the studio to make sure our guests had arrived. I checked the new set we had designed, shook hands with everyone and huddled with my team to make last minute changes to the script

As we finalized details, it was easy to feel a shift in energy as the Mayor walked in, captivating onlookers with his polished style, muscular build and trademark shaved head. As he worked his way through the crowd, the Mayor's crisp white shirt, silver cufflinks and gray pinstripe suit created a perfect complement to the set's new décor. It was times like this that I cherished his dedication to his own looks.

"Good morning," he said, smiling and shaking hands as he walked toward the makeup artist who had been waiting patiently for his arrival.

I stood next to him as makeup was applied to his light brown skin. "Button up," I reminded him as I dusted off the shoulder of his jacket.

"Here's the fashion police," he murmured while taking his cues. I quickly scanned his face. Born in the late 1950s, Ray Nagin's youthful features conveyed confidence and conviction.

"Don't forget to thank the shipbuilders for continuing to operate in New Orleans," I instructed as powder hit his shiny bald head, "and recognize Lieutenant Bodet from the State Police for his great work on the Contraflow plan."

"Got it."

"And 'Bo-day' is the correct pronunciation of his name," I added.

Most of the time the Mayor relished my direct comments, knowing they were geared toward his success. He challenged me, however, if I seemed too eager to appease a conflicting faction.

"Don't make me look weak, Sally," he would caution. "You're too kumbaya."

Having come from the private sector as a vice president of cable company Cox Communications, Ray Nagin always spoke his mind, including his honest take on the good and bad in New Orleans. For many local citizens, electing him represented a chance to rid City Hall of cronyism and alter the landscape in a place known for harboring political corruption.

Louisiana, often called a banana republic, ranked high in the number of elected officials convicted of crimes. Former Louisiana Congressman Billy Tauzin was said to have joked, "Half of Louisiana is under water and the other half is under indictment." In 1991, then-Governor Edwin Edwards ran yet again for re-election against a former head of the Ku Klux Klan named David Duke. Edwards, who had been indicted three times but never convicted, won the race with bumper stickers that read, "Vote for the Crook, It's Important." Both Duke and Edwards later went to prison, Duke for mail and tax fraud and Edwards for racketeering, extortion and fraud.

Nagin also experienced the corruption first hand. While campaigning, he was offered a Louisiana lunch – cash in a brown bag – and firmly declined it. Upon becoming mayor, Nagin opened the doors of City Hall to the FBI and Department of Justice, resulting in federal investigations targeting former city officials. The Mayor himself ordered an investigation into the city's Taxicab Bureau and Utilities Department and was told that his own cousin would be implicated in the scandal.

"If he's guilty, arrest him," he said.

Images of officials from the Taxicab Bureau being led out of City Hall in handcuffs impressed a citizenry tired of Louisiana politics. This also served the Mayor his first slice of significant national attention. A headline in *The Atlanta Journal Constitution* declared, "New Orleans embraces Nagin – First-year mayor is all business in war on corruption."

By attacking corruption, the Mayor showed that he didn't mind stepping on a few toes to clean up the image of the city. "I'm an equal opportunity toe-crusher, Sally," he would often say.

Seletha Nagin captured her husband's motivations best when responding to a complimentary e-mail I forwarded to her:

Good morning Sally!

You know when Clarence came to me and told me he was thinking about running for mayor, my initial reaction was that of shock and a feeling of fear ... But after the shock, came a calm.

This is a man who never had any political aspirations and even said he would never get involved in politics! When I realized he was serious, I knew it wasn't about me, it wasn't about him, it was about making this city a better place for ALL citizens.

Clarence is a GOOD, HONEST, CHRISTIAN man who didn't have to take on the huge challenge but out of all the men in the city we sincerely believe that a higher being felt like he was the one to do it.

Because it was time for a change. Time for our city to get back on its feet and be the city it should be.

Clarence puts himself on the line every time he opens his mouth, but you can believe that whatever he says comes from the heart and is well thought out before it comes out because he loves this city and all the people in it and wouldn't do anything to hurt anyone.

Seletha

This attack on corruption also represented the Mayor's style of politics. Averse to courting political relationships, he often consulted only a small circle of advisors while making policy. As a result, politicians on both sides of the aisle frequently complained about the Mayor's lack of contact. "Let's just create the right environment for projects to succeed without interference from City Hall," the Mayor would say as a guiding principle, proving he was less likely to abuse the power of his office but also less likely to use that power to make government processes work to their full benefit.

This political isolation represented Ray Nagin's Achilles' heel: enormous distrust of politicians and their agendas. Once, I had encouraged him to put together a "kitchen cabinet" of advisors, people he wanted to emulate, who could provide guidance and support on difficult issues.

"Who would you put on this?" he asked.

"College presidents, former mayors," I suggested.

"Same old, same old," he retorted, eliminating further conversation on the matter.

As with any elected official, the Mayor heard frequent complaints, but his overall distrust of others caused him to interpret many situations as personal attacks, as in an e-mail I received from him about Gene Schreiber, President of New Orleans' World Trade Center:

> Read the CAFTA *(Central American Free Trade Agreement)* article this morning. The comments that caught my eye were from Gene. Tell him I am not happy about his comments directing me as mayor to make phone calls. Tell him if he is not happy with what I am doing with international then he can count on less support going forward. Can't wait to see him.
>
> MN (Mayor Nagin)

I played kumbaya and tried to explain that there was no ill intent in Gene's comments, but it did little to ease the wound.

"I grew up in the Fifth Ward," the Mayor told me, referring to his working-class neighborhood. "When you got hit, you hit back."

Nagin's popularity, however, was not affected by his independent streak. With approval numbers in the 80s, his self-assured persona soared.

In his earlier years, while attending Tuskegee University on a baseball scholarship, Ray Nagin had earned a degree in accounting, highlighting an interest in details and analysis. As a chief executive, he became a careful observer who did not like the burden of timelines or deadlines, evaluating all aspects of a project before acting.

"Let's let this percolate," he often said.

As a team leader, the Mayor frequently promoted people from within City Hall, preferring dedicated loyalists who could be trusted in his battle to victory. He likened his team to an army of renegades fighting the good fight and described his views in an e-mail to me: "Someone once said a small band of revolutionaries can change the world. You're part of our band. Let's change New Orleans for the better."

The Mayor gave his lieutenants the leeway to do their job but would jump in quickly if he felt loyalty was being compromised. As a result, members of the executive staff treaded carefully when making decisions. "Just do what you think is best and ask for forgiveness later," former Chief Administrative Officer Charles Rice advised me. "That way, at least something is getting done."

However, the Mayor was passionate about his speeches and talking points, considering them one of his most important tasks to manage. "I want a good open and a strong close and a new nugget of information each time," he would urge. Our writing team was well aware of the Mayor's style and worked hard to craft the right words for his delivery.

"What's the take-home here?" he would ask while scanning for the hook in a draft of talking points. If it wasn't catchy enough for the Mayor, we went back to the drawing board or recycled his standard idioms: "We're at a tipping point now," or "If there's one thing you remember from my speech, buy a piece of dirt in New Orleans."

The Mayor abhorred "political speeches" that sounded canned and hated to read from a script. Most of his speeches were written in bullet points, appropriate at times except when details were critical. He worried more about punch than substance in his words, feeling a strong need to leave a lasting impression with memorable ideas. All too often, that lasting impression was delivered with slang or words intended to play to his audience.

Speaking to a group of students one afternoon, he described a person as "ballin'."

"What on earth is ballin'?" I asked him later.

"Someone who is rich or doing well," he responded.

"Just say 'doing well' next time," I begged.

"Don't make me speak all English," the Mayor retorted, feeling pushed toward language that was too "proper."

"Let the audience rise up to you," I answered. "Be a statesman with your words."

Months after the hurricane, speaking to the National League of Cities, the Mayor asked mayors around the country to urge Congress to fund the rebuilding of New Orleans. "Everyone knows there's a certain amount of constipation in Washington," he said. "We need to be the Ex-Lax to bust through that."

Immediately after these gaffes, the media wanted comments on the Mayor's comments, to which I wanted to reply "no comment" to defuse the original comment.

"No need to be glib, just stay mayoral," I fussed at the Mayor.

But he still used the podium to throw punches and often let the audience know that I would not approve. "Sally's going to need the smelling salts for this one," was a proverbial line.

The Mayor was at his best when he opened up about his personal life and his past, but he was not comfortable doing so. At a press conference for a food drive, he stood at the podium and recounted often splitting a single chicken between his family of five, with the breast being reserved for his father, who among other things worked as a janitor at City Hall. "Why don't you talk about that more?" I pressed.

"I don't want to go there," he said.

I was not going to press him on this one.

Back in the office on the Thursday before the storm, I received word about an exciting announcement for the city. Donald Trump planned to build a new Trump Tower in the business district, giving New Orleans its biggest skyscraper yet. Greg Thomas, *The Times-Picayune* real estate reporter, had been granted an exclusive story by the developers and would be breaking the news soon.

"Wake up!! Trump story is for Friday, A1," he wrote, denoting its placement on the front page of section one. "I'm told this will be the most spectacular building New Orleans has ever seen. Please get me the mayor and please help me keep this under wraps until Friday morning paper."

Greg wasn't the only reporter in need of the mayor's time; our afternoon schedule included several other interviews with local reporters. For these media rounds, the day's topics included saving our city's naval base, a proposal for crime reduction, the Mayor's recent trip to Brazil and what was shaping up as a potential cakewalk to a second term.

The day ended without a single question about the weather.

Meanwhile, across the Gulf of Mexico, a tropical storm off the coast of Florida was upgraded to a hurricane named Katrina. The storm hit Florida, eventually killing 11 people.

Chapter 1

Gumbo Zeb

Friday, August 26

After looking up at the sunny sky Friday morning, I unfolded the newspaper and scanned the headlines. "You're hired!" was in the lead story about Trump along with the Mayor's quotes positioned throughout the article. I scurried back inside the house in my fuzzy pink slippers as Barq's howled through the window.

"Here's the story," I said to my husband, Ron, as he added heavy cream to his coffee in the kitchen. "What do you think?"

"It's a good sign for the city," he said. "And it might give us the boost we need to finally develop the riverfront." As President of the Audubon Nature Institute, Ron had built a downtown aquarium and park on the edge of the Mississippi River.

"Let's go, kiddos," I urged the children as they leisurely got ready for school. "Don't forget anything, either, Mr. Absent Minded Professor," I reminded our 13-year-old son, McClain. We piled in the car after kissing Ron goodbye.

"What a beautiful day," I said while turning on the radio for some light music.

"Mom, do not sing," replied 14-year-old Cassidy, in her typically joyous teenage whine of protest. I dropped the kids off at school and headed downtown to City Hall.

"Audrey, did you see your quotes?" I asked our head writer, who was pregnant with her first child, upon my arrival. Several media outlets had used her headline in their stories.

"Yes," she laughed as her cheeks blushed, eluding the attention.

In my office, I turned on the computer, checked my messages, grabbed a pen and made my daily lists of things to do. On my morning calendar was preparation for the city's annual budget hearing, a meeting to choose gifts for an upcoming women's conference, design approval for the next cover of our *One New Orleans* magazine and an executive staff luncheon at the downtown Hotel Monaco.

Storm's Intensity	Wind Speed	Water
Category 1	95 miles per hour	5 foot surge
Category 2	110 mph	8 foot surge
Category 3	130 mph	12 foot surge
Category 4	155 mph	18 foot surge
Category 5	Greater than 155	Total destruction

I quickly scanned my favorite news sites on the web, and then clicked on the tropical weather section of Wunderground. Now in the lower Gulf of Mexico, Katrina was a Category 1 hurricane on the Saffir-Simpson scale. I looked at the scale:

Almost every forecast associated with the storm called for it to intensify in the warm Gulf waters and double back before hitting the

Florida panhandle. In New Orleans, we always kept an eye on the weather, but this storm did not seem to be headed our way.

After a busy morning, I headed to our executive staff luncheon at Cobalt Restaurant in the Hotel Monaco. The team consisted of the Mayor and the nine people who ran the city's primary departments, excluding police and fire. The Mayor had designed the get-togethers to encourage solidarity on the executive staff.

With conflicting personalities and priorities, it didn't always work.

I felt honored when I became a member of the executive staff and took my responsibility to the city seriously. I was rooted in New Orleans through both sides of my French and Spanish Creole families. My great-grandfather, Dr. Paul Gelpi, inventor of the Gelpi forceps that are still used today to deliver babies, had begun a family tradition of nine children. When my parents had their nine, I was the sixth. Needless to say, we were Catholic.

In my pink baby book, in the section marked "Where I was born," my mother skipped the name of the hospital and wrote in bold red ink, "Independence, Missouri." While still small, my father moved us to an unincorporated area outside of New Orleans called River Ridge. Born between three brothers, I was as comfortable in a tree house as I was in a dress. Long skinny legs that resembled stilts under my 5'9" frame garnered me "Stickly," one of several nicknames I would carry through the years.

Upon taking my first communications course in college, I knew I had found my calling. I had always asked endless questions so my dad began to call me "Ba-ba Wa-Wa" for Barbara Walters. Later, I became the news director for KLSU, LSU's campus radio station, before obtaining my degree in broadcast journalism. I became the assistant public information officer in the Louisiana House of Representatives and then a press aide in the Louisiana Governor's Press Office.

Like many people in the South, I grew up in a family of conservative Democrats. Boll weevils in the South voted for Republicans and Democrats, following the candidate's ideals or personality, not party affiliation. "Vote for whichever candidate is best, regardless of their party," my dad would frequently say.

A few years after working in the Governor's office, I met and married Ron Forman, New Orleans' zoo director. A talented manager, Ron's love of nature had inspired his successful career. In the 1970s, with a small group of committed volunteers, he turned the dilapidated Audubon Zoo into one of the leading zoos in the country. After we married, I spent several years at home raising our children and volunteering in the community.

In the late '90s, I re-entered the workplace and opened a small speakers bureau with Michele Carrere. Being back at work was challenging and intellectually stimulating. In 2002, the director of the city's Office of Economic Development, Beth James, asked me to join her team as chief of protocol. An excitement was brewing around Mayor Nagin in his efforts to change the culture and dynamics of City Hall, so I accepted the job offer.

In my new position, I served as the official host for visiting dignitaries, the city's liaison to the Consular Corps and the coordinator of sister city agreements. I also ordered flags, packaged gifts and executed proclamations.

My first day on the job brought an unexpected twist when I ran into the Mayor. "What are you doing here?" he asked as I saw him at a city-sponsored event.

"Working for you," I answered, assuming he would have signed off on the hire.

"For who?" he asked again, as if he had not heard.

Whom, I thought. "You," I said.

"Doing what?" he asked.

"Protocol," I replied as shock registered on his face. I had met the Mayor on a few occasions and perhaps was known best to him as the wife of a public figure.

His shock quickly subsided as I delved into my work. New Orleans had begun losing consulates but was still considered a major international port city. I rolled up my sleeves to lend support to the dedicated international business community at the World Trade Center and Port of New Orleans, which was trying to reinvigorate the city's efforts to retain our standing as the "Gateway to the Americas." We waged an uphill battle while Houston, Miami and Mobile gained ground.

Working for city government revealed a strange lesson: being a city appointee often meant being placed on a pedestal. I tried to remind people who would go out of their way to accommodate my every whim that, "we work for you."

Later, when asked to head up the city's Communications Department, the Mayor asked me to retool the office. "You are a person who operates at a high level of excellence," he said. "I need your perspective."

It didn't take much for me to bite.

Now ready for lunch, I sat at the end of the table in the private room at Cobalt Restaurant and waited for the rest of the group to arrive. Colonel Terry Ebbert, a veteran Marine and the city's director of Homeland Security, marched in on slightly bowed knees and polished shoes. With the air of a dapper grandfather, he removed his fedora, revealing a cropped head of salt and pepper hair over steely brown eyes.

"Sally, I need to talk to you," the Colonel said as he gestured me closer. "The military event that the Mayor missed caused a big problem for us." I glanced at the eagle on his Marine Corps ring, reminding me that he would not tolerate minimized support of the military by the administration. "He's got to do better."

"We don't know the priority events," I replied. "Pick four of the most important events in the year covering all of the military branches and I will get them on his calendar."

As director of Homeland Security, the Colonel served as the city's liaison to police, fire, emergency services, military and emergency preparedness. The Homeland Security department was burdened with several limiting factors: a staff that was too small, infighting with the technology department over grant money for interagency communications and complex plans not fully understood by many other departments and agencies.

"We are herding cats with multiple departments and agencies," Colonel Ebbert said after one training exercise, "in a complex evolution loaded with potential for mistakes."

To augment his capabilities, the Colonel developed strong ties with the regional FBI field office, giving him entrée into special security sessions at FBI Academy in Quantico. There, he learned how to keep a keen eye on terrorist cells hoping to attack vulnerable targets in the United States. As a major tourist destination, New Orleans' main threats involved port security and managing large special events like Mardi Gras. But in 2004, a Pakistani national had been arrested in Charlotte, North Carolina, with surveillance videotapes of transportation lines and government buildings in New Orleans.

"I have shown the video to all necessary folks and taken all required actions," the Colonel assured me when reporters called.

Back inside the restaurant, I ended my conversation with the Colonel just as the Mayor walked into the room and took the empty seat on the other side of me.

"What's going on?" he asked.

"I'm just getting an update from the Colonel," I said.

On the other side of the Mayor sat Greg Meffert, the city's Chief Technology Officer. A portly techie with blazing blue eyes hidden behind flowing bangs, Greg was a left-brain genius who had invented software in a garage during the dot-com era and made it to the big leagues. Now he was delivering key successes for the administration, such as putting city services like paying parking tickets and taxes online and developing the first high-tech network of crime cameras in the city.

But in front of the camera, Greg's garbled delivery sometimes made him seem unintelligible. "And, you know, every time we're like okay, okay, it's going to happen, it's going to happen," he mumbled in one interview.

And although administration policy called for interviews to be cleared by my department, Greg often ignored this.

"When did he go on and why did I not get a heads up?" the Mayor asked me after one of the many unexpected interviews. "Greg is not our best spokesman on a consistent basis. You must get control of this."

As the waiters served lunch to Greg and the rest of the executive staff, we got down to business that Friday over typical New Orleans fare – spicy mirliton soup with lump crabmeat, shrimp Creole over fresh redfish and hot French bread.

The conversation started out light and I complimented Kenya Smith, our impeccably dressed Director of Intergovernmental Affairs, about his elegant suspenders. Soon matters became more serious as Finance Director Reggie Zeno mulled over the upcoming budget hearings in the City Council chambers with Don Hutchinson, our Economic Development director. Reggie and Don were longtime bureaucrats who understood the angst that could be associated with budget hearings.

While the discussion continued, I drifted on in thought about an irate message I received earlier from a person in New York. "The phrase 'The Big Apple,' was coined by African American stable hands from New Orleans," said the angry man. "New York continues to claim this phrase as their own and the Mayor of New York isn't properly addressing this."

"What do you want me to do?" I had asked.

"Pass an ordinance or a law demanding that New York no longer use this term without the appropriate recognition for these stable hands," he said. I had moved this message into my "X" file.

As the discussion bubbled around me, I turned my head in the direction of my three female colleagues, Chief Administrative Officer Dr. Brenda Hatfield, City Attorney Sherry Landry and Housing Director Alberta Pate. Brenda, a graceful woman who rarely raised her voice, was the most trusted by the Mayor, having worked with him at Cox Communications. Sherry, who often challenged the Mayor on legal issues, was by far the most intelligent on our team. Alberta was the hardest working in a room full of workaholics.

There we were, five African Americans, five whites, from different schools, backgrounds and geographic locales, like a big bowl of gumbo zeb. The Mayor prided himself on our diversity and the unique perspectives we brought to the table. I, too, loved the medley we created with different chords and tunes. We were Democrats, Republicans, Independents, academics, liberals, conservatives and centrists. I thought of my large family and knew that growing up with eight siblings could help me navigate this kaleidoscope of people, power, personalities and perspectives. And by navigating the team, I could better learn to navigate the city's most sensitive challenge: race.

In a city with almost 70 percent African Americans, racial and economic problems had fed an undercurrent of cynicism for a long time. Since 1978, when Ernest "Dutch" Morial became the first African American elected mayor, the increasing black population and subsequent "white flight" almost guaranteed black leadership in government to address the problems. For people from poorer neighborhoods, many of them African American, black leadership did not alter the perception that life was unfair and that government was the body that could, would and should fix their ills.

The Mayor would often point out how this disenfranchised group of poor, uneducated African Americans might interpret a decision by saying, "We might think this is the solution but poor black folk will say this…." Often the only Caucasian in the room, I learned to better understand the plight facing this group and how to more effectively communicate to them.

Some of the opinions presented to me were hard to grasp: "O.J. should be cleared even if he was guilty because rich white people hire powerful lawyers and get off all the time," or "black Republicans are never to be trusted." But I used the time to listen and learn, probing and prodding the divergent points of view, reminding myself that I wasn't poor, I wasn't black and I had never walked in their shoes.

In the restaurant, waiters served more hot French bread. Our conversation turned upbeat as we discussed no formidable opponents appearing in the upcoming mayoral election just eight months away. But the Mayor resisted the notion of an easy win. "I don't want to just get re-elected," he said. "I want to go in with a big mandate."

With his support from the white community intact, the Mayor talked about locking up more support from the African American community. According to conventional wisdom, many blacks felt abandoned by Nagin for allowing the federal government to explore possible wrongdoing in the administration of former Mayor Marc Morial, a man greatly admired by the black community.

"They're all mad that I would do this to a brother," he had explained to me.

"What if someone in his administration had really committed a crime?" I asked.

"That doesn't matter to them," he had answered.

This contradiction left the Mayor feeling conflicted. "If I do something the white community likes, the blacks get upset, and when I do something to help the black community, the whites get upset," he often grumbled. "I'm in this constant tug-of-war."

Adding fuel to the fire was a New Year's Eve incident during which an African American college student from Georgia was killed at Razzoo's, a nightclub on Bourbon Street. Mug shots of the suspects showed four white bouncers, whom witnesses accused of suffocating the young man after a skirmish. Allegedly, the victim didn't adhere to the club's dress code, but many people pointed out that white men wearing similar clothing had been allowed inside.

The Mayor directed his Human Rights Commission to investigate charges of racism on Bourbon Street. He began the process with a press conference to announce that "mystery shoppers" would patronize Bourbon Street bars. The results of the study were appalling, revealing that 40 percent of clubs were still charging African Americans higher prices for drinks than whites.

Responding to a request from a wealthy liquor distributor to meet with the Bourbon Street club owners, the Mayor fired off an angry response.

> Let me just forewarn you, I will not tolerate blatant racism in the City of New Orleans during my watch. I am really pissed that after giving the bar owners plenty of advanced warning that they still did not have their employees sensitized. My advice is to get your customers on Bourbon Street to clearly understand that this is not going away unless they clean their act up. We will continue to monitor until they get it right. The next time we will publish the offenders and seek whatever legal and/or punitive action necessary. For Christ sake this is 2005!

Soon after the study was released, the Mayor called me into his office. "I'm concerned about black people taking to the streets in a riot," he said. "Read this."

As I took a deep breath, he handed me an editorial by publisher Ed Lewis of *The Louisiana Weekly,* an African American newspaper. "Regardless of what lies ahead," Lewis wrote, "the challenge for people of color in this city is to cling tightly to the faith of our forebears and to commit to doing whatever it takes to throw off the shackles of bigotry, privilege and discrimination by any means necessary. Let's get free or die tryin', y'all."

The Mayor wasn't afraid to challenge people on both sides of the race issue and lashed out at a black activist whom he felt crossed the line. "There are so many people who constantly play the race card when they can't get what they want," he wrote. "My advice to you is to please stay in San Francisco for a while and get the blinders from your eyes and the hate out of your system."

Race, politics and economic development had become a part of every major executive staff discussion and this day was no different. As we wound up our lunch, my Blackberry began ringing. Our press secretary, former television reporter Tami Frazier, was on the phone with a weather update. I thanked her for the call and hung up. Turning to the Mayor, I said, "You need to comment on the storm named Katrina when we get back."

"What's she doing?" he asked, using the female vernacular.

"She's just a Category 2 way down in the Gulf," I said, "heading straight for the Florida Panhandle."

Two of the four local television stations met us for comment at City Hall upon our return. The Mayor faced the cameras. "We are watching the storm and I encourage everyone to start their initial hurricane preparations," he said. People in New Orleans knew the drill: stock up on water, canned food, batteries and flashlights, put gas in the car and get cash from the bank. After the impromptu press conference, I headed upstairs.

The far right corner in the executive offices on the second floor of City Hall housed the heartbeat of the Communications Department, the writing team and press office. Audrey Rodeman and Lesley Eugene, our two senior writers, were busy drafting. Audrey's eyes were affixed intently on her computer while she adjusted her chair to accommodate her pregnant belly. In the adjacent office, Lesley placed her nervous hands on her temples while editing her work. Across the hall, Press Secretary Tami Frazier stared at her notes with penetrating eyes while her long black hair covered a phone in each ear.

"I'm setting up the bumps," she whispered, referring to interviews for the Mayor.

I stood in the doorway as Deputy Director Terry Davis, or TD as we called him, walked toward me. At 6'4", TD was an eccentric who would shy away from contact with people, bewildering reporters. "How can the deputy director of Communications have an answering machine that does not accept messages?" I was often asked.

"Because he's good," I would answer, pointing to TD's unique ability to craft slogans, including terms such as "Hollywood South" and "One New Orleans."

In Audrey's office, she drafted our next press release while the team crowded at her computer for weather updates, concern appearing on several faces. Suddenly, a new advisory emerged from the National Hurricane Center, moving the storm track a tad westward from the previous prediction.

"This mother freaker could hit us," I said. The staff laughed, used to my twisting curse words into less vulgar expressions. Every now and then, if the real word came out, I quickly followed it with an "Excuse my French."

Audrey got up and rubbed her big belly as she walked over to the dry erase board that kept track of pending projects in our department. With her blonde hair bobbing, she erased all of the assignments off the board and wrote, simply, "Hurricane." The room got quiet.

"We have a lot to do right now," I said, snapping back to attention. "Let's go."

I moved quickly down the hallway to turn in my list of essential staff to our fiscal officer, securing five rooms at the Hyatt Hotel across the street from City Hall if the storm headed our way.

Later that afternoon, the National Hurricane Center issued an advisory forecasting that Katrina would soon be a Category 3 hurricane that would make landfall somewhere along the Florida/Alabama coast, approximately 250 miles east of New Orleans. The Governor declared a state of emergency for the state, but we were still in the clear.

After work, the kids went out with their friends and Ron and I had dinner with Margaret and Ken Beer at Clancy's, a local favorite. The restaurant was packed.

"Isn't it strange how this restaurant is full and how few people here seem aware of this storm?" Margaret asked. "Can you pass the fried oysters, please?" Ron said, more interested at the moment in the food.

Ken, an oil company executive, had already evacuated his offshore rigs and was receiving Blackberry updates on wave heights in the Gulf of Mexico.

"What's the latest in the Gulf?" I asked him. "Is everybody cleared off the rigs?"

"Absolutely," he answered. "This storm could really hurt production and have a devastating effect on gas prices." Ken was typically so calm that my antenna went up.

"What else is bothering you?" I asked.

"We've never seen a storm so wide and massive," he added somberly.

As we ate our dessert, the waiter offered up his best hurricane joke. "Why are hurricanes named after women?"

"I don't know," I answered.

"Because they're wild when they arrive and take your house and car when they leave."

"That's not funny," I said with a smile.

Chapter 2

Premature Evacuation

Saturday, August 27

I woke up to a typically sultry day in New Orleans with hot temperatures and heavy humidity. It was Saturday morning, the day many people ran errands and headed to parks and playgrounds for weekend football and nectar snowballs. I checked my e-mail and read the 5 a.m. advisory from the National Hurricane Center. Just our luck, forecasters were now placing New Orleans in the middle of Katrina's cone of uncertainty as a Category 3 major hurricane.

"This could get ugly," I said to Ron. "Maybe you shouldn't stay at the zoo this time," I added, pointing out the latest satellite image on the computer.

Ron's hurricane plan called for sleeping on the top floor of the reptile house with a few other dedicated zookeepers at the Audubon Zoo, above the giant anaconda, king cobra and pygmy rattlesnakes. Life preservers, tranquilizer guns, rifles, provisions for the animals and staff and a small skiff were all they would have.

"I'm not leaving town if I'm asking the staff to stay," he replied. "The most I will do is stay with you and the kids at the Hyatt."

"That works for me," I said. "Now let's start battening down the hatches." We walked through the back yard of our home, packed up hoses and garden tools, and then tossed the lawn chairs into our pool. In the front yard, we checked on power lines, cleared our catch basins and storm drains of debris and talked to neighbors gathered on the street. After having faced several false alarms during previous hurricane alerts, no one appeared overly concerned.

I arrived at City Hall to see storm preparations fully underway. Chief Joseph Matthews, the soft-spoken new director of the Office of Emergency Preparedness, and his tireless assistant Soraya Guirreri, monitored the weather. The Mayor called a meeting for the executive staff, as well as for the heads of police, fire, emergency services, health, water and emergency preparedness, to take place right after our morning conference call with the National Hurricane Center.

I walked through the offices of the Communications Department. With her long black hair in a ponytail, Tami sat in her office and answered several phones at a time. Audrey dashed in and out of offices, working hard to release the latest information to the public while holding her pregnant belly like a ball. Nervously monitoring the breaking news, Lesley sat at her computer and typed away, only turning to look at her young daughter's framed picture. TD paced up and down the halls, going into the restroom to wash his hands several times, his idiosyncratic nature in full view.

I moved into the Mayor's office and took my place at the conference table, extra chairs now in place so that everyone had a seat. The mood was subdued as we checked the big screen television in the corner for updated information on the storm's track.

The Mayor walked in through the private back door entrance dressed in a short-sleeve golf shirt, as if he would be in the office for a while. He threw his sports coat onto a lone black leather chair near his desk, said hello and took a seat at the head of the table.

"Yesterday they thought this storm was going to hit Florida or Alabama. Now it's looking as if we're the target," he told the team gathered around. "This could be the one we've been dreading – so we need to be more than ready with every aspect of our work."

We all nodded in agreement.

"Sherry, we need to call a mandatory evacuation," the Mayor told City Attorney Sherry Landry.

She contemplated her response. "There is no precedent for this," she answered, "so it's going to take time to make it happen because of the legal issues involved." Typically, several bureaucratic procedures had to be carried out prior to the enforcement of a city government directive. "We particularly have to work out how we handle the hotels," she added, provoking a discussion centered on whether or not hotels could be forced to evacuate their guests.

"Just do it," the Mayor answered tersely.

He turned to Colonel Ebbert. "Colonel, what do you have?"

A methodical planner, the Colonel discussed the readiness of the Office of Emergency Preparedness and Emergency Medical Services. It was obvious this job was already requiring tremendous resolve on the Colonel's part as he began to check off a list of each department's responsibilities.

As the Colonel spoke, I checked my own official responsibilities within the city's comprehensive emergency management plan. When assuming my job, I had read the plan and had a clear understanding of emergency and disaster operations, but I picked up the manual to reread the sections that pertained to me.

The coordination of public information is a shared responsibility of the Office of Emergency Preparedness and the Office of Communications. Public information procedures are divided into three phases: continuing education, pre-disaster preparation and post-disaster recovery.

1. Develop adequate educational materials for dissemination to the public prior to the disaster.
2. Coordinate and develop all news releases to be delivered by elected officials, and consult with other city departments and agencies in development of appropriate bulletins affecting their activities in which the public must be informed.
3. Literature in the form of pamphlets, flyers, circulars, etc., will be made available for public distribution. The literature will cover all aspects of emergency and disaster response.

With press releases going out regularly and interagency activities coordinated, I had this covered, I thought. Little did I know that in the storm's immediate aftermath I would fail miserably at number 3.

The Colonel wrapped up his comments and passed the torch to the emergency preparedness director. "I'll start with evacuations," Chief Matthews began. "The Superdome will be used as a shelter of last resort for both special needs patients and the general population. We'll open up first thing tomorrow morning just for special needs patients." I rapidly took notes to give to Audrey and Lesley so they could release the information. "The Louisiana National Guard will be running the operation there for us."

"We have a couple of hundred National Guardsmen," added the Colonel. "They will help process the people as they arrive."

"What else is happening with the special needs patients?" the Mayor asked. "Are they all just going to the Dome?"

"No," said Dr. Kevin Stephens, director of the city's Health Department. "The state has set up some shelters and we are using several special needs buses to take patients to Baton Rouge. Once we fill up the buses, we will start putting people in the Dome." As a former medical director of Charity Hospital, an institution founded in the 1730's to provide health care to the city's poor, Doc stephens was focused on the indigent.

Suddenly, Doc changed the subject. "I have been working on plans to put people on buses, trains and barges to evacuate but we haven't finalized these plans," he said. The room became quiet. Two things seemed strangely out of place: why was our health director discussing transportation out of the city when that was clearly a task of the emergency preparedness office, and why hadn't these transportation modes been finalized earlier? Recognizing that the position of emergency preparedness director had sat empty for several months, I hoped Chief Matthews, as the new director, would take this over from Doc Stephens and make it a top priority. Though Doc continued to discuss barges, his comments were soon dismissed since no plans had been fully established.

I scanned the room to find Dr. Juliette Saussy, director of emergency services. The blond-haired spitfire was bright and a doer, and I became curious when I didn't see her.

Water Board Director Marcia St. Martin then briefed the Mayor on staffing at the city's pumping stations. A petite but tenacious woman with vital knowledge of the intricate drain lines and pipes feeding the city's treatment plants and pumping stations, Marcia seemed to be executing a fully developed plan.

"Contraflow will begin at 4 p.m.," the Colonel resumed. Contraflow, the state's process of phased evacuations, forced all Interstate lanes into a single, outbound direction so citizens could evacuate storm-prone areas. "The lower-lying parishes have already begun evacuating and it's all going smoothly according to the state plan."

Chief Charles Parent of the New Orleans Fire Department then calmly detailed the Fire Department's readiness. "We have equipment spread all through the city, preparations are underway at all of the station houses and we'll have personnel on duty throughout the storm," he said, exhibiting no outward signs of worry about the terrible events to come. A gentle leader, Chief Parent had recently walked a tightrope between the Mayor and the firefighters' union regarding back pay, generating tremendous respect from those who had observed his efforts.

The Mayor checked his list to see what he had missed. "We need to talk more about our plans to send the buses throughout the neighborhoods tomorrow to pick up people who have no means of evacuating." A look of concern covered his face. "How many buses do we have?" he asked.

"About 15," Chief Matthews answered. "They will transport all day from schools and centers throughout the city to the Superdome."

"Eddie," the Mayor said, looking at police Superintendent Edwin Compass, "can your officers use loudspeakers to alert people in the neighborhoods to the locations of bus pick up-points?"

"No problem," the Chief answered like a proud soldier.

But problems were already surrounding the chief of police and the Mayor had shared his concerns in an e-mail to me months earlier: "My gut is telling me Compass will blow this big time," he wrote about a new plan the Chief had proposed for crime fighting. "He comes out with a new initiative every month and I think he is quickly losing credibility in both the white and black community. Not sure he will make the journey with us to the promise land."

As we wrapped up the meeting in the Mayor's office, we again covered the details of arrangements regarding buses. "Brenda," the Mayor said to Chief Administrative Officer Brenda Hatfield, "we need to call the City Council and make sure they know about the pick-up points in their district." Brenda jotted down the Mayor's directive like a pupil in a classroom.

"OK," she said, the pen still poised on her notebook.

"Make sure they're on board with this," the Mayor added in a rare show of political inclusion. "And let's call the criminal sheriff and lieutenant governor, too."

"I'll take Sheriff Gusman," said Kenya, standing and smoothing his shirt.

"Sally, will you take the lieutenant governor?" asked Brenda.

"Sure," I answered. We split the remaining calls and everyone exited the office to organize his or her department's storm preparations. I stayed in the Mayor's office to go over the media requests coming in from national and local outlets.

"What time do you want to do the next press conference?" I asked.

"Let's plan on 1 o'clock," he replied. "I'll call the Governor and let her know." He pressed the speakerphone button and dialed her office.

"Governor, how are you?" After exchanging pleasantries, the Mayor provided an overview of the morning. "I just had my staff in here going over preparations and we are going to hold a press conference in just a little while."

"I'd like to be there when you do it," the Governor replied. "I will be coming in a little later in the afternoon."

He whispered to me, "Can we change it to 2:30?" I nodded approval and he confirmed the time slot. "2:30 is fine, Governor," he said.

"Governor, there's another issue," the Mayor continued.

"Yes?"

"I spoke to Aaron Broussard this morning and I think he's going to jump the gun again by issuing an evacuation for Jefferson Parish before it's his time," the Mayor said, referring to the parish timeline in the Contraflow evacuation plan. On the phone earlier, Jefferson Parish President Broussard told the Mayor, "I am not going to leave my citizens with only one day's notice to evacuate."

"Governor," the Mayor continued, "I think you need to know this so that it doesn't cause a problem on the highways."

"Did you hear that?" the Governor asked someone on her end of the line. "Broussard's going to jump the gun again."

Earlier in the year, during a false alarm evacuation for Hurricane Dennis, Broussard ordered residents to evacuate before their scheduled Contraflow time, causing needless delays on the Interstate. He was subsequently accused of causing "premature evacuation."

"I am going to come in and talk to him," the Governor said. Originally from the Cajun Country of Lafayette, Governor Kathleen Blanco was a consensus builder, and she would need her refined political attributes to iron this out.

I leaned back in my chair, pleased to see the Mayor and the Governor working so closely together. Their relationship had been strained since the Mayor had endorsed Blanco's Republican opponent, Bobby Jindal, in the 2003 race for governor. Like several other Democratic loyalists, Blanco was stung by the Mayor's perceived desertion of the party.

"Let me tell you what the Governor did, Sally," the Mayor had explained to me one day. "She called me during the governor's race and told me I had better not go against her. But I had asked both Blanco and Bobby what their plan for the City of New Orleans would be. She came back to me with a short letter while Bobby presented this big, well-thought-out plan for the city. When I read Bobby's plan I knew that that was the kind of person I wanted to work with – I didn't care what party he was, he just had the right plan. Blanco and [Senator Mary] Landrieu gave me all this party crap."

The Mayor and the Governor's relationship had been hot and cold since then, but aides from both camps were working hard to repair it. In one such instance, we visited the Louisiana capitol to tape an interview with the Governor for the Mayor's television show. Our staff developed closing questions for the Mayor that could suggest warming relations, such as, "What has it been like being the first female governor of Louisiana?" and "What do you love most about New Orleans?"

After the Mayor completed his interview, he took me to task for posing such lob-ball questions. "That was bor-ing," he pined. "Don't make me do something like that again." True to form, Ray Nagin did not like political scripting.

Today, however, the Mayor was partnering closely with the Governor to secure the lives of citizens. In her amiable "Aunt Bee" style, the Governor was immediately responsive to the more approachable Mayor, recognizing the need for his full cooperation to successfully handle the emergency.

Up the chain of command, the White House also worked collaboratively by ordering federal aid for relief efforts along the Gulf Coast. The President's official action authorized the U.S. Department of Homeland Security and its sub-agency, the Federal Emergency Management Agency (FEMA), to coordinate disaster relief efforts and to provide assistance for required emergency measures. Authorized under Title V of the Stafford Act, these measures were meant to save lives, protect property and secure public health and safety. Representing the federal government was Michael Brown, undersecretary for emergency preparedness and response, and William Lokey, FEMA's federal coordinating officer.

I was roaming the City Hall second floor hallway, from the press offices to the Mayor's office to the pressroom, when suddenly the smell of hot pizza filled the corridor.

"Mama mia, I'm famished," I said to Audrey. "Let's eat."

The Governor arrived in New Orleans with key staff and her strapping husband, Raymond, a former college football instructor nicknamed "Coach." She and the Mayor greeted each other genially. While Coach sat down to eat, the Governor offered warm greetings to everyone in the room. Like a favorite grandmother, Kathleen Blanco made sure each and every person was touched. Other officials gathered inside and outside the Mayor's office waiting for the press conference to begin.

The pressroom was packed as our entourage filed in, the Mayor and Governor leading the pack. At the podium, the Mayor struck a tone befitting the gravity of the situation. "This is not a test. This is the real deal," the Mayor began, adding urgency to the news he was delivering. "Things could change, but as of right now, New Orleans is definitely the target for this hurricane. We are following the state evacuation plan," he explained, "so that residents in low-lying areas can leave first. We want you to take this a little more seriously and start moving — right now, as a matter of fact.

"We will open the Superdome as a refuge of last resort. If you plan to go there," he instructed, "do not bring weapons – they will be confiscated – no large items either. And bring enough food for three or four days, just to be safe."

The Governor moved to the microphone to address evacuation shelters being set up in Tallulah, Vidalia, Bunkie and throughout Louisiana. "We have sent a letter to the President requesting federal assistance," she said. "But we need each of you to be prepared." While she spoke, the Mayor stood on his toes behind her with a confident air, nodding at reporters to gauge their reaction to his earlier statements.

Chief Compass approached the podium to address curfews and public safety. "Looters will be dealt with severely and harshly and prosecuted to the fullest extent of the law," he said. The press conference finished after nearly an hour.

Later, a meeting was held to update essential City Hall staff in the City Planning offices on the eighth floor. Director of Public Works John Shires, Director of Sanitation Veronica White, Director of Recreation Charlene Braud, Deputy Chief Administrative Officer Cynthia Sylvain Lear, the Colonel, Brenda and the Mayor ran through their checklists. A news crew tried to get into the meeting but was kept at bay by Audrey, who was winded from both the pregnancy and quickly running up the stairs. The meeting wrapped up with most department heads fanning out onto the streets to secure playground equipment, traffic signs, city vehicles and public buildings.

At 4 p.m. Saturday, with Contraflow in full effect, all lanes of Interstate 10 headed outbound. Across the street from City Hall, Press Secretary Tami, writer Lesley and our photographer, Shane, checked into their rooms at the Hyatt. Downtown New Orleans appeared eerily quiet.

An hour later, the Mayor hit the airwaves. "I have issued a voluntary evacuation and urge all people who can leave to leave," he stressed. "I have declared a state of emergency and our legal team is working to determine if we can order a mandatory evacuation without exposing the city to liability," he said. "So tomorrow, you may have the first mandatory evacuation of New Orleans."

When the newscasts ended, I received a note from Gordon Russell, an investigative reporter who covered City Hall for *The Times-Picayune*. "Sorry to bother you with this at this juncture, but the paper just called me and wants me to find out a bit more about the city's plans for those who can't evacuate," he said. "Like, for instance, is there any plan to use RTA buses to ferry people out of the city?"

I'll punt this one to Colonel Ebbert, I thought, who, having worked alongside Lieutenant Colonel Oliver North during the Iran-Contra hearings, would have the ability to handle the question.

The storm would hit before he had a chance to do so.

At home Uptown, we relaxed in the family room while gray clouds loomed over the trees in our back yard. With the day's work completed, Ron and I decided to spend the quiet evening going to a movie.

"How about Jodie Foster in 'Flightplan'?" I asked.

"As long as it's not one of those 'shoot everybody blood and guts' movies, I'm fine," said Bambi-lover Ron.

At the theater, we munched on popcorn in the nearly empty rows. During a tense scene, I shielded my eyes from the screen. My Blackberry buzzed. It was 8:08 p.m. when an e-mail came in from the Mayor. "Confidential – just talked to the head of hurricane center and he is very scared for us," he began. "The storm surge could be as high as 20 to 25 feet, which would top levees by a lot. He says lots of people will die."

"Jesus, Mary and Joseph," I gasped. Ron turned toward me.

"I checked with Sherry and she said we could do a mandatory," the Mayor's message continued. "My question is should we go hard tonight or in the morning?" he asked, wondering how we should relay this to the public.

"We have to leave now," I whispered to Ron.

After running to the car, I wrote back to the Mayor, "It's way too important to not strongly encourage action tonight." The Mayor would need to share the warning from Max Mayfield of the National Hurricane Center and force action without creating widespread panic. "The message needs to be very serious and somber (i.e. I am very, very concerned that each and every New Orleanian hear the seriousness of this message)," I typed furiously on the Blackberry.

When Ron and I arrived home, I jumped in my car to meet up with the Mayor at the television stations.

"This is a very serious storm," the Mayor said into the cameras, delivering the message as succinctly as possible. "Come the first break of light in the morning, you may have the first mandatory evacuation of New Orleans."

Following the final interview, we stood in the parking lot as the Mayor outlined a plan to try to evacuate more people. We would draft a letter and fax it to churches before morning services to encourage the implementation of a buddy system for those needing help evacuating.

I called Audrey, and she and Lesley composed the letter. "Dear Religious Leader," the letter began, "Hurricane Katrina is now approaching New Orleans and puts us in imminent danger. We need everyone's help to keep the people of New Orleans safe. I ask that you use any church vehicles to help move your members out of harm's way. This is a time when we must turn to our faith and come together as one New Orleans to weather the storm."

The Mayor edited the letter. "Add 'encourage your members to adopt a senior citizen or a family that relies solely on public transportation' and make sure the letter fits on one page."

I made it home after 11 p.m. to see Ron glued to the television.

"Well, your warnings worked," he said. "All of the stations have been talking about the Mayor's comments. If that didn't convince someone to leave, nothing will."

I spent most of the night at my desk revising the church letter and working to get it faxed.

Unfortunately, because of problems with the distribution list it never went out.

Late that evening, I looked over the mandatory evacuation order that legal-eagle Sherry drafted for our review. It stated:

> A mandatory evacuation order is hereby called for all of the Parish of Orleans, with only the following exceptions: essential personnel of the city; essential personnel of regulated utilities; essential personnel of hospitals and any patients that are not able to evacuate; essential personnel of nursing homes and any residents that are not able to evacuate; and essential personnel of the media and essential personnel of operating hotels and any hotel patrons that are not able to evacuate. Unless covered by one of the aforementioned exceptions, every person is hereby ordered to immediately evacuate the City of New Orleans or, if no other alternative is available, to immediately move to one of the facilities within the City that will be used as refuges of last resort.

Audrey called my house at midnight as she finalized the clergy letter. "Sally, I think I should evacuate but I don't want to leave you here," she said wearily.

"You're PREGNANT … go!" I said. In the middle of the night, Audrey hit the road. Knowing most hotels did not allow pets, she slipped her cat, Scoopa, inside a duffel bag.

Concluding my work, I sent Lesley some notes for the Mayor's next press conference. "For his talking points, include the bus pick-up locations, the Dome opening at 8 a.m. for special needs patients, midday for the general population and the church letter that we are going to fax."

I walked upstairs to check on the kids, who were sound asleep. I kissed them quietly. Slipping into bed, the clock read 2:15 a.m. I tried to sleep, but was too worried about people who were not evacuating.

I thought back and realized that growing up I had never evacuated for a storm. When storms approached, Mom cooked while we put water in our tubs, canned goods near the stove and flashlights with extra batteries in every room. Back then, it was customary for people to go to a nearby school or community center for shelter, but the Red Cross no longer set up shelters below Interstate 10. And in more recent times, many people still did not evacuate because they were elderly, ill, without transportation, without means or cautious about protecting their homes from fire or looters.

And for the die-hards, it was a chance to throw a hurricane party.

Chapter 3

Put on Your Alligator Skin

Sunday, August 28

The situation became dramatically worse overnight as Katrina catapulted in just hours from a 3 to a 4 to a 5 on the Saffir-Simpson scale. The unnaturally warm loop current in the Gulf of Mexico had caused the storm to spiral into ferocious winds of 175 mph.

I woke up, grabbed the paper and immediately checked the website of the National Oceanic and Atmospheric Administration. "Katrina," forecasters Richard Knabb and Richard Pasch wrote, "now a potentially catastrophic category five Hurricane. Coastal storm surge flooding of 15 to 20 feet above normal tide levels ... locally as high as 25 feet along with large and dangerous battering waves ... can be expected near and to the east of where the center makes landfall."

"Everybody up!" I screamed throughout the house.

"Why are you waking me up this early? That's evil," shouted my daughter Cassidy, with the vengeance of a teenager who hadn't gotten enough sleep.

"This is a very serious day," I hollered back upstairs, adding sage advice from my father. "I need you both to put on your alligator skin and tough it out."

I worked quickly on the morning's press release that would announce the mandatory evacuation and again remind people about evacuation procedures. "Citizens are advised to: fill their cars with gas, remove potential debris from their yards, board windows and glass doors, make sure that nearby catch basins are clear of leaves or trash, stock up on bottled water, batteries and non-perishable food items, check on family, friends and neighbors, especially the elderly, to make sure everyone has an evacuation plan and make provisions for pets."

I headed downtown absorbed in thought, thinking about the buses that were now picking up people throughout the city. At the first major intersection near my house, crowds of people had parked their cars on the neutral ground, or median, of Claiborne Avenue and were boarding buses for the Superdome.

As I neared City Hall, I puttered slowly in my car, amazed at the scene in front of me. Throngs of people headed into the Louisiana Superdome while National Guard assisted the police by checking bags and searching for contraband. People teemed in, coming from every possible direction around the Dome, and I grabbed my camera to record the crowds.

At City Hall, we gathered in the executive offices on the second floor and the conference room near emergency preparedness on the ninth floor.

"Here are pictures I took outside the Dome," I showed the Mayor. "It looks like a Super Bowl crowd right now."

Tami prepped the Mayor for the morning press conference. "Most crews are going live," she said, as she tightenel her ponytail.

"Good," the Mayor said. "We need to use this press conference as our final chance to ratchet up the alert for people to evacuate."

The Mayor understood how to skillfully use the media. Earlier in the year, however, he had allowed his emotions to overpower this skill during our annual State of the City address, a municipal task comparable to the President's State of the Union address. A draft was developed for the Mayor, with input from key advisors. The Mayor tore the draft apart, dicing and slicing it word by word.

"What message do you want to convey if you didn't like any of these?" I had asked.

"I want to talk about what's going on by asking residents if they really know what time it is in this city," he said. "Let's build a theme around time."

"OK, then we'll delete the weather," I said, referring to his earlier decision to use sunny and cloudy skies throughout the speech.

"Also, Sally, I want to knock the media for that recent story and cartoon," he said.

"Mayor, we have such positive overall press," I told him. "Just tell them what you think in private and leave it out of the speech."

"They need to be called on their stuff," he argued.

"That article could have been much worse, and it comes with the territory of being mayor," I argued.

"I want to make them think about crossing the line," he stated.

"You're only giving them more to write about," I said, firmly holding my ground.

"Sally, remember to let Ray Nagin be Ray Nagin," one of my colleagues suggested as we left the room. "If he attacks the media in the speech, at least we will know what he's saying. Otherwise, he will say it later in a speech we can't control."

Inside City Hall, the Governor arrived as she did the day before but with a bigger entourage. The head of the Louisiana National Guard, Major General Bennett C. Landreneau, and Colonel Henry Whitehorn, head of the Louisiana State Police, walked shoulder to shoulder with her. The Governor again graciously made her rounds.

"The mandatory evacuation is ready," the Mayor informed her. "We're all set."

"Good," she replied. "I just spoke with President Bush and told him you would be calling the mandatory evacuation." The police and fire chiefs, criminal sheriff, members of the City Council and other officials crowded around. Before exiting the Mayor's office, everyone prayed.

In the pressroom, national and international reporters stood side by side with the local press corps. The Mayor stood tall and approached the podium. "Good morning. I wish I had better news, but we're facing the storm most of us have feared," he announced with dramatic calm. "This is going to be an unprecedented event so today I am ordering a mandatory evacuation of the city of New Orleans."

The Mayor looked at the cameras in the pressroom, taking note of the larger number. "This morning the Superdome has already opened for people with special needs. If you have a medical condition, if you're on dialysis or some other condition, we want you to expeditiously move to the Superdome," he said. "Then at noon today, the Superdome will be opened as a refuge of last resort, where we will start to take citizens that cannot evacuate. But I want to emphasize, the first choice of every citizen should be to leave the city. The Dome is likely to be without power for days after the storm, but this is still a better option than staying home."

According to the mandatory evacuation order, staying at home was now technically a violation of the law, albeit one that the police would not be enforcing.

While the Mayor spoke, Bob Mann, the Governor's communications director, stood next to me. "There are Spanish radio stations in the New Orleans market," I whispered. "Don't forget to keep them abreast."

"I will, thanks," he said in his affable style.

The Mayor held his papers to make sure he had covered everything. "If you do stay in your home, don't forget an ax to break out of your attic," he added. "If we galvanize together I'm sure we can get through this."

As the Governor got up to speak, the Mayor stepped to the rear. "We are expecting intense flooding that is beyond our control," the Governor said. "This storm is following the predicted track so it's important that we all get out."

Bouncing on tiptoes, the Mayor assessed his performance while smiling and winking at people seated in the audience.

"You did just fine," I would tell him later.

After the press conference, our team checked in with each other. Not sure if I had received the latest weather report, Lesley got up from her writing desk and cried out to me, "Did you hear? It's a Cat 5!"

Rounding the corner, I could see the fear in her face as well as others who overheard what she said. "I know," I answered as reassuringly as possible. "No need to be afraid though. You'll be safe at the Hyatt."

I walked outside to see what was happening at the Dome. The lines outside were now snaking far into the street. A heavyset man walked by me pulling a large green garbage bag along the sidewalk, his elderly mother and two small children in tow. I looked up at the clouds. It had begun to drizzle.

"Sally, the reporters want to know what we are doing to get those people out of the rain," Tami said when I came back inside City Hall.

"Tell them we are making sure they're safe once inside the Dome, and that means checking each one in individually," I replied. "Hopefully, they will not get too wet from the rain." She jotted down the response.

On the Interstate outside, Contraflow was in full effect as more than one million people evacuated. The National Weather Service issued an unprecedented warning forecasting incredible human suffering at about the same time that Max Mayfield of the National Hurricane Center briefed the President.

The Mayor made one more trip to local television stations as we announced a 6 p.m. curfew. The Governor released another statement urging evacuation. "I am gravely concerned about reports coming in regarding those who are choosing to not evacuate. I strongly urge you to get to safety while there is still time to do so," she said.

"She's talking about a cultural change here," I whispered to Tami.

"And wasn't the Dome trashed last time people went there?" Tami asked.

"Yes," I said, "during Hurricane Georges in 1998, the first time the Dome was used as a refuge of last resort, some people inside caused thousands of dollars worth of property damage."

As we huddled in the office, we received word that three nursing home residents had died after becoming dehydrated on their evacuation bus. I became mindful of something that Audrey had said earlier: "Remember, even preparations for a storm can have a devastating ripple effect on people."

The Colonel and Chief Matthews were now positioned in the emergency center at City Hall. With his Marine ring on his finger, the Colonel laid out a post-storm battle plan: "If there's flooding, our first priority is search and rescue, but we're flying as soon as possible to assess the damage," he said. "And we've got the support of 4,000 National Guardsmen mobilizing in Memphis right now."

"What about the numbers at the Dome?" I asked.

"We have between 10,000 and 15,000 people inside," he answered. Media reports indicated there were 30,000 people when the doors finally closed, but no accurate count was ever performed.

As soon as our work was completed, I headed to the Hyatt to meet Ron, who had checked in with the kids and our nervous cocker spaniel, Barq's. Ron and McClain wrestled on the hotel bed while Cassidy lay in the adjoining room watching television. Barq's barked relentlessly at the boys.

"Mom, tell them to stop," Cassidy said, as I walked in the room. "I can't hear the television."

"Let's just close the adjoining door here, Petunia," I answered, hoping to keep the peace. I looked at Ron with a crooked eyebrow as if to say, "You take her, I'll take him."

In the lobby, the Mayor roamed the hallways. Two solidly built New Orleans police officers, Louis Martinez and Wondell Smith, loomed as bodyguards behind him. Having sent his family to Dallas, the Mayor moved freely on the fourth floor of the hotel as it began to serve as a staging area for city employees.

Greg the techie set up computers in the Burgundy meeting room on the fourth floor, determined to tackle any communications problems that might arise.

"Dude, we're set," he told the Mayor, pointing to equipment stationed near the long rows of cots.

Like a seasoned schoolteacher, Brenda calmly chatted with elected officials and executives from Entergy, the local utility company, who had set up their command center on the Hyatt's fourth floor.

I checked in with various officials but saw no immediate needs. Down the hall, a small group of storm reporters had crammed into a pocket-sized corner room. I said hello to those I knew and introduced myself to the others: Brett Martel with The Associated Press, Erika Bolstad with the *The Miami Herald*, Charlie Varley of *The Guardian (UK)*, Scott Gold of *The Los Angeles Times* and Joe Gyan from *The Advocate*, Baton Rouge's daily. I worked hard to accommodate reporters' individual requests, but kept a slight distance from the media to support the Mayor's more detached style.

Around the corner in the Burgundy Room, some of the Police Department's top brass threw their belongings on top of the cots. Other officers remained at police headquarters and district stations throughout the city. At the Superdome, tall and commanding Deputy Chief Lonnie Swain held down the fort with a few hundred members of the Louisiana National Guard. Across town, Brigadier General Brod Veillon and other National Guardsmen waited at the low-lying Jackson Barracks.

Later that evening, our family had dinner in the Hyatt's atrium restaurant with friends Kristi and Erik Johnsen, who had opted for a "vertical evacuation" at the downtown hotel. The Johnsen clan included two children and two dogs. Cassidy and McClain were thrilled to be eating dinner in a restaurant with Barq's, whose typically skittish behavior was now bordering on neurotic, and two other dogs. After a nice meal, we went upstairs to our rooms and settled into bed.

Approaching midnight, the hotel alarm sounded. "You must evacuate your rooms," came a voice through the public address system.

"Come on," Ron said. "We have to get out of here now."

"What's the problem?" I asked.

"I'm sure it's the windows," he answered.

Downstairs, thousands of people filed into the hotel's ballrooms, while we headed for a practically bare fourth floor meeting room reserved for city personnel. As we rolled out our sleeping bags and lay down next to the kids, howling winds blew out hundreds of windows on almost every floor.

Chapter 4

Death Calls

Monday, August 29

"We can't sleep," Cassidy grumbled, as she and McClain rolled toward me on the blue cotton sleeping bag. "He snores too loud." Cassidy pointed to a heavy-set man sleeping on his back on a nearby blanket. I placed pillows over her ears to rectify the problem, but they failed to buffer the noise.

"OK, let's try another spot," I said. We moved to a nearby conference room and found a vacant corner for our makeshift beds. Across the room I spotted Scott Domke, one of Greg's technology employees, and police Chief Compass, sitting with his wife, who was eight months pregnant. City Council members and other officials were also in the room with their families and staff.

The Mayor, Brenda, Chief Compass, Greg and I huddled periodically to receive our news. At 4:30 in the morning, we received an e-mail from Colonel Ebbert in the emergency center at City Hall. "All is well as can be expected," he began in Marine-like assessment. "The Dome still has power, police power and communication are out but City Hall power is up," he said, adding "the building is swaying like a cruise ship."

I checked on the location of the eye of the hurricane. The storm would officially make landfall at 6:10 a.m. in Buras, Louisiana, 57 miles south of New Orleans, with waves as high as 47 feet reported on the offshore buoys.

"Guess what?" Chief Compass asked as the two of us waited in the same room where our families now slept. "Today's my birthday."

"Really?" I asked. "What day is today?"

"August 29," he answered.

"Dang, it's my birthday, too," I said, having not even remembered my own birthday.

"Can you believe today is my birthday?" he asked again, making me wonder if he had even heard that we shared a birthday. "The exact day this storm hits."

Promoted as a cop's cop, the talkative and expressive commander had dreamed of being police chief ever since he was a young boy growing up in a rough section of New Orleans. Schoolboy charm and a desire to succeed complimented his mix of African American and Hispanic roots.

"My grandmother taught me Spanish," he had told me, "but I couldn't let anybody know."

"Why not?" I asked.

"They'd beat you up if they thought you were trying to be smart," he said.

Chief Compass was warm and friendly, often greeting people with a handshake and bear hug. But a climbing murder rate, a Police Department plagued with allegations of corruption and an unhappy mayor had begun to put pressure on the Chief.

At the Mayor's direction, I had begun the discreet task of helping spruce up the Chief's public image. After a few staff meetings on how best to approach this, we decided to produce a 30-minute police show for public television. We set up a preliminary production meeting in Chief Compass' office.

After requesting old photographs to use in the show, the Chief lit up when showing off pictures of his family. Soon he was tooting his own horn as he described the numerous awards on his wall and the famous people he knew. "Here's a picture of me with Steven Segal," he said. "We're great friends."

"He's seems so insecure," one of my staff members said as we left the meeting. The meeting had made me more aware of the Mayor's concerns, but I was still unsure how to give this brash commander a public relations makeover.

Now at daybreak on Monday, the morning of the storm, many of the police Chief's top lieutenants stood next to me in the Hyatt. Like an Eagle Scout, Captain Marlon Defillo commanded public information for the Police Department. With broad shoulders and a poised demeanor, Marlon maintained his natural composure as his trusted deputy, Paul Accardo, worked several communication lines. I watched as Paul worked quickly, his pale skin and black hair framing dark, protruding eyes.

Inside the hotel, windows continued to rupture and shards of glass sprinkled everywhere. Crouching down, I peered up into the atrium lobby. Pieces of the ceiling were beginning to fall. Gazing outside, the building now resembled the Alfred P. Murrah Federal building after the Oklahoma City bombing.

"Don't get too close," said Louis, one of the Mayor's powerfully built bodyguards, as I leaned over the balcony. At 6'4", Louis offered an air of fortification.

"I won't," I answered. There to protect the Mayor, Louis and his partner Wondell also watched out for those of us who worked closely with their boss.

Sneaking away to a higher floor in the Hyatt, I could see the Dome's roof flapping in the wind, undoubtedly causing water to pour into the building. We knew flooding might occur in the city since so much of our land stood below sea level, but I wondered how we would handle a flooded Superdome.

Still morning, the Colonel updated us on calls coming in from residents. "We've got people on rooftops and clinging to trees," he said. "Even though the storm took a slight turn to the east, we've still got water topping a levee at the Industrial Canal, water in the Ninth Ward and water in New Orleans East," he said.

To prevent flooding in low-lying areas, an intricate levee system had been built in New Orleans decades ago, aided by a series of drains and pumps designed to push water out of the bowl that formed the city. But levee topping would create more floodwater than our pumps had the capacity to drain.

"At least one building has collapsed," the Colonel said. "We have at least five fires, and at Charity Hospital windows have blown out."

I sat next to the Mayor and jotted down notes. "This isn't good," he said to me.

"How are buildings collapsing?" I asked.

"Maybe the wind, maybe the water," he answered.

"We need to update the press when you're ready," I said. We dialed in to the "Today" show. Matt Lauer began the interview saying, "Luckily, New Orleans may be spared the worst-case scenario that had been feared."

The Mayor responded by admitting, "Well, we're still not out of the woods as it relates to that worst-case scenario. As a matter of fact

I've gotten reports this morning that there's already water coming over some of the levee systems. In the Lower Ninth Ward, we've had one of our pumping stations to – to stop operating."

As we huddled on the fourth floor in the late morning, we received a report about a levee breach at the 17th Street Canal in Lakeview, an area completely across town from the Ninth Ward and New Orleans East flooding. In the emergency center, Capt. Mark Willow reported the breach as a 20-foot break. The challenges were now coming like stampeding wildebeest.

Across town, as soon as the storm winds allowed them to, members of the National Guard surveyed the damage downriver in Chalmette near Jackson Barracks. Hearing a thunderous roar, they looked to see a wall of water coming their way. They ran inside to the second floor of the barracks. It was later determined that the water rose 12 feet in just 40 minutes.

At the 911 call center inside police headquarters, the pleas for help came in quickly throughout the morning. Deputy Chief Warren Riley reported 600 calls within the first few hours. The 911 operators would later describe the conversations as "death calls."

> **Caller:** Yes, 911, help...
> **911 operator:** Where are you ma'am? How many are inside the location with you?
> **Caller:** Right now I got a handicapped girl and I got a baby that's on the pump machine ... the baby's on a ventilator, but he's in a bed and the water's coming up.
> **911 operator:** How old ... the baby is an infant?
> **Caller:** Yeah, the baby's 8 months.
> **911 operator:** And you have a handicapped son?
> **Caller:** I have a handicapped sister.
> **911 operator:** A sister?
> **Caller:** Yeah.

911 operator: And that's just you, the baby and your sister inside the house?

Caller: No, and my son, and my daughter, and my son-in-law, and my brother. One, two, three, four, five, six of us a baby...

911 operator: OK, ma'am what we need you to do ... we need you to get to higher ground until we're able to get to you ...

Caller: We're up on the sofa in the front room ...

911 operator: You need to get to the, um, do you have an attic inside your home?

Caller: No.

911 operator: You don't have an attic?

Caller: Uh-uh.

911 operator: OK, well you need to get to higher ground, OK? Even if you have to get up to the, uh, to the roof, but I need you to get to higher ground.

By late morning, flooding calls increased, as rising water became a crippling concern. Fires caused by broken gas lines sprouted up in destroyed homes and buildings. Emergency personnel waited anxiously for the wind to die down so they could begin the monumental task of saving lives.

"Twenty buildings have now collapsed," the Mayor said.

"Where?"

"I'm not sure, but one is a small apartment complex."

Chief Compass came in. "We've already had to arrest looters," he said.

"Are you kidding me?" I asked incredulously, knowing hurricane winds were still upon us. "Has the wind died down enough for me to cross the street?"

"Not yet," he answered.

"What's happening at the Dome?" the Mayor asked Chief Compass.

"I'm going to let people go outside onto the ramps later to get some fresh air," he answered, wiping sweat from his brow. The lack of power and sanitation had already created a stifling environment.

"That's a good idea," the Mayor replied, his white T-shirt still clean, but now wet from sweat. "They're probably all hot and dirty."

Doc Stephens reported on the infirm. "We've been busy with the young, old and everything in between with exhaustion, heat stroke, chest pain, people who forgot their medicine, diabetes, you name it," he recounted.

FEMA Director Michael Brown arrived in Baton Rouge and issued a statement urging out-of-state first responders to "remain where they were" so that the response could be properly coordinated, while in Washington, President Bush made emergency disaster declarations to free up federal funds. But the President then continued with other work, going to a senior center in California to discuss new Medicare prescription benefits.

I walked over to Marlon, who held a police radio trying to get reception. "What do you think?"

"I don't feel good about this," he whispered, departing from his usually optimistic nature.

Frightened, I quickly changed the subject. "Don't run yourself ragged," I said, patting his broad shoulder.

"You either," he replied.

Marlon knew I would roam the streets without the protection of a weapon. "I want you to take this," he said, like a Scout leader helping a Brownie, as he handed me a police cap embroidered with a large law enforcement insignia. "Just don't lose it."

"Thanks," I replied warmly, tucking it in my purse.

I walked over to his deputy Paul, whose dark Italian eyes were now filled with worry. "Paul," I said, "Marlon gave me his hat."

"Be careful out there," he warned.

By late afternoon, I walked across the street, the wind and rain still churning as thick mountains of clouds covered the sky. On Poydras Street, the main artery between City Hall and the Hyatt Hotel, debris littered the ground. I carefully placed each foot down to avoid stepping on glass. At the corner, a blown-out Bank One branch sat with an exposed bank vault and teller stations.

Once inside City Hall, I ran into Marcia from the Water Board and fire Chief Parent, whose forehead crinkled over his eyes. "Is everything OK?" I asked, suspecting that unreachable fires throughout the city, including a 5-alarm blaze at the Southern Yacht Club, were disturbing him.

"This levee breach in Lakeview is big, Sally, over 200 feet long," the Chief answered. "This could cause Lakeview to be completely under." Evidence of a 200-foot breach was devastating and I thought about the horrific impact this would have on our city. "I have it confirmed from some of our own firefighters," he added.

"Damn," I replied. "Marcia, what do you know about it?"

"We are trying to get out there to check it out," she said.

I passed on the grim news to the Mayor. "The breach is the cement wall portion about 200 feet long past Old Hammond Highway."

"There goes another chunk of the city," I mumbled, petrified of the horrors now facing us.

Monday evening, our executive staff gathered at City Hall to meet with Marty Bahamonde, FEMA's public affairs liaison. Gathered around the ninth floor conference room table, Bahamonde explained the devastation he had just seen in an aerial tour of the city. "There's water everywhere," he reported. Confirming our earlier reports, he said the hardest-hit areas appeared to be the Lower Ninth Ward, Lakeview, Mid-City and eastern New Orleans.

Councilwoman Cynthia Hedge-Morrell echoed the FEMA representative's concerns after riding through parts of District D, which she represented.

As the meeting came to a close, Sherry talked about legal issues while she diligently compiled a list of items that the city would need from the state and FEMA. The Mayor would later recount this exercise to reporters. "FEMA said 'give us a list of your needs,' and let me tell you, we gave them a hell of a list."

After our meeting, Bahamonde used the phone to call FEMA officials in Washington to report his findings. In later testimony to federal investigators, Bahamonde stated that he tried desperately for 16 hours to communicate the urgency of the situation to FEMA officials in Washington. This testimony would contradict FEMA Director Michael Brown's allegation that he wasn't aware of the grave conditions in the city for days after the hurricane. Senator Joe Lieberman, then the senior Democrat leading the investigation, said, "This disconnect is beyond disturbing. It's shocking."

After meeting with FEMA, I drafted a flyer to communicate with people inside the Dome. "Disaster Update," it read. "Help is on the way." Nowhere did I make note of levee breaches or the severity of flooding in the city to avoid inciting fear and panic in the thousands of people inside. With Audrey evacuated, I asked several colleagues to review the flyer for edits.

"Shane," I then said to the staff photographer, "insert one of the photos from my camera onto this flyer and then make 10,000 copies downstairs." Our printer sat in the basement of City Hall.

Shane took the finished piece and walked down the stairs to the print shop to produce the copies. A little while later, he reappeared. "The printer's not working," he said. "There's no electricity down in the basement."

"See if you can find another printer that works," I said. I would soon realize that had I properly planned for the emergency, I would have secured a small printer and generator. Now, direct contact inside the Dome would be our only access to evacuees.

The Mayor drove over to WWL-TV, the only station still on the air, in his black Rambo-style SUV that was lovingly nicknamed "Big Daddy."

"Eighty percent of the city is under water," he reported in early evening coverage. "There's an oil tanker that has run aground and is leaking oil, you see flames sparking up from the water and we have buildings that look like a bazooka was shot through them," he added, graphically describing events from the day.

I suddenly realized it was getting late so I left City Hall to track down my family at the Hyatt. I could not locate Ron, Cassidy or McClain anywhere. "Has anyone seen my family?" I asked several people while roaming the halls and floors of the hotel.

I came across Linda Meffert, Greg the techie's wife. "Ron took off hours ago with the kids," the petite brunette replied.

"Why didn't he tell me?" I asked out loud, sure that Ron was trying to get the kids to a safe place, but frustrated that he hadn't let me know.

I walked to my car and drove my SUV out of the City Hall garage to head home. When I reached St. Charles Avenue, I quickly realized my error in judgment. Known for its canopy of oaks, the majestic avenue was now blanketed with fallen tree limbs. I edged along the impassable streets and medians, but debris blocked every major intersection and side street. The night was pitch black except for my headlights. I drove over massive branches and skirted around power lines that still twisted in the wind, cursing up a storm while hoping I wouldn't get electrocuted or wind up with a flat tire.

It wasn't long before I became trapped by large branches. I stepped outside of my car and began to haul them away to clear a path. A police officer finally drove up. I followed him up and down side streets, weaving in and around debris. It was two hours before I made it home.

When I entered my house, votive candles lit the foyer. "Ron, Cassidy, McClain?" I shouted. Voices carried from the rear of the house.

Like a good dog, Barq's ran up to me. In the kitchen, the Johnsen children held flashlights while searching for unspoiled food, Ron having obviously brought them here from the Hyatt.

"Where are Cassidy and McClain?" I asked Britt, their young daughter, whose red hair bore a resemblance to Little Orphan Annie's.

"Upstairs," she answered.

In the family room Ron, Kristi and Erik sat on the couch, trying to gather news from a portable radio. I plunked down next to them.

"What do you think?" Erik asked.

I was tired and scared and shocked and mad but could hardly speak. I answered vaguely, suddenly realizing that their home had probably washed away. I did not want to be the one to tell them.

"It's not good," I said. "I'm afraid a lot of people may have died because there's water almost everywhere."

I went to bed wondering what more we could have done to make people leave.

Cassidy and McClain prepared for vertical evacuation to the downtown Hyatt Hotel.

Barq's was the first one ready to evacuate.

Members of the Communications department worked feverishly, from left, me, press secretary Tami Frazier and writers Lesley Eugene and Audrey Rodeman.

Hordes of people teemed into the Dome on Sunday, August 28, 2005.

New Orleans had at least seven levee breaches that flooded 80% of the city.

As the storm passed, (from right) Col. Terry Ebbert, Chief Charles Parent, Chief Edwin Compass and Entergy CEO Dan Packer updated Mayor Nagin in the Entergy command post.

Daily media briefings were conducted with a small pool at the Hyatt.

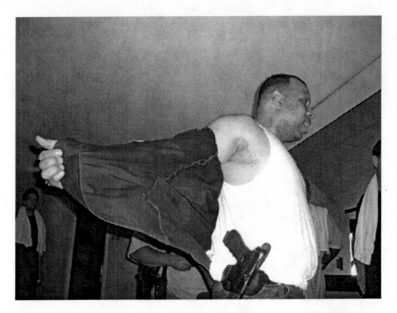

New Orleans Police Chief Eddie Compass came in from the fray.

Public Information Officer Capt. Marlon Defillo responded to non-stop emergency radio calls as Entergy CEO Dan Packer and the Mayor listen in.

The Hyatt hotel, where we bunkered down,
was devastated inside ... and outside.

XXXL boxer shorts, some of the loot commandeered for law enforcement.

The "human chain" formed by Chief Compass Wednesday night to secure provisions.

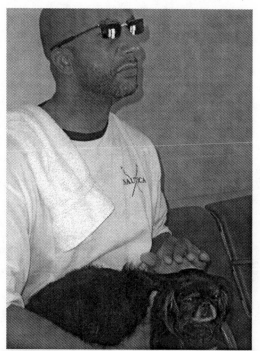

A lost dog found the Mayor while bodyguard Wondell Smith was followed by another stray.

Trapped at the Dome.

The sick gathered at the Dome.

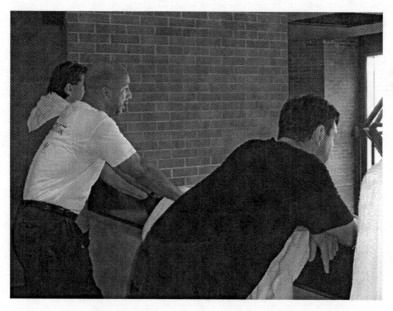

Greg the techie, the Mayor and Ron looked onto
the swelling Dome crowds from the Hyatt.

Chapter 5

The Bowl is Filling Up

Tuesday, August 30

The next morning, the Johnsens piled their two young children and two anxious dogs in the back of their truck in an attempt to reach their home. "Be prepared for the worst," I said.

As Erik drove toward Claiborne Avenue, Kristi later told me she spotted a dead body floating in the water. "Alex and Britt," she said quickly to her children as she pointed in the opposite direction, "look over here."

"We can't let them see this," she had whispered to Erik, staring at him in fear.

At daybreak, I walked outside as I did every morning in my pink fuzzy slippers, but this time not with a coffee mug and not in my heavy chenille robe. Our neighbors, Julie and Parker LeCorgne, were outside. Parker was stubborn and did not want to leave, worried about abandoning his family's 100-year-old business, Dr. Tichenor's, located in now-flooded New Orleans East. Julie, having grown up in the

Bahamas and aware of the effect of killer storms, was exasperated. "Sal, see if you can convince him to leave."

"Parker, there's nothing you can do about the East now," I said. "It's mostly under water and people are being rescued from the flooding there."

"That look of anxiety on your face might be the only thing that can get me to leave," he said. As they exited the city, the LeCorgnes would be hounded by a long checkpoint delay where rescuers had begun dropping the rescued and the dead.

An hour later, Cassidy and McClain woke up sweating in the un-airconditioned house. Temperatures were in the 90s and New Orleans' famous humidity was in full force. With my obligation to the city, I packed their overnight bags before Ron drove them to my sister Mary's home in Lafayette. Ron plotted the trip knowing the journey would be long, but determined to have our children welcomed into the safe, loving arms of family.

I locked our dry, fairly undamaged home, got back in my SUV and headed downtown, navigating through tree limbs and power lines once again to meet up with my colleagues. Ron had provided a maze of directions for me with streets that were still dry and more passable.

As I drove up onto the Interstate toward the city's center, I suddenly began weaving around people stranded on the elevated expressway to seek higher ground. An elderly woman trudged barefoot along the overpass, dragging a bulging canvas bag with a tattered blanket hanging out. Ten steps behind her, two young men in white shirts and low-riding jean shorts walked slowly, a hint of panic in their eyes.

I knew we had to help all of these people, but wondered if we had enough resources to effectively respond. I kept driving and could see water engulfing the city ahead. As I inched forward, a group of young children, two girls and one boy, gathered on the side of the road with no adult in sight. I jumped out of the car.

"Are you okay?" I asked the oldest girl, whose pink shorts were sopping wet. She appeared to be around eight years old.

"We can't find our momma," she said.

"Come this way," I said, as I walked her to a policeman positioned twenty yards ahead. As we walked over to him, the little girl grabbed the hand of the younger boy and girl.

"Hold hands, ya'll" she said, mothering the other children light-years ahead of her time. The policeman put them in his car.

Further along the Interstate, I got out of the car to survey the water. Looking under the bridge, I noticed a man floating face down, his middle section buoyed while his arms and legs hung down. I wondered who he belonged to and if we would ever know.

As I drove back toward town, I saw a city vehicle out of the corner of my eye. Suddenly, I could see Brenda and Tami in the car so I waved them down.

"Where are you going?" I asked, rolling down my window.

"The Mayor has told all senior staff to get out of town," Brenda explained like a teacher hurrying pupils to safety during a fire drill.

Tami quickly rolled down the back window, her black hair now pulled up in a bun. "I'm leaving, Sally-Wally," she said, fear all over her face. "I'm scared here."

"If you feel like you need to go, by all means go," I said. "I'm going to find the Mayor."

As they drove away, I sat in the car and looked out on the flooding, a tragedy beyond epic proportions. Ahead, a big-nosed man with a square jaw walked slowly, his face tattered in tears. I began to panic for the city and everyone in peril, wondering how in the hell we would help everyone who needed it. My fear began to intensify, then I heard my father say, "Sally, put on your alligator skin."

Dad's right, I thought, if I let myself feel this man's pain, I won't be much good to anyone. And from that moment forward, I went back to work, plugging emotions that had no place in emergency response.

I continued down the Interstate. A small group of people in FEMA shirts stood perched on the highrise facing the Dome. Good, I thought, the cavalry has arrived for their mission.

I put on the police cap that Marlon had given me and pulled my ponytail through the velcro in the back. As I descended the Interstate ramp, I screeched on my brakes and stared at the road ahead. On the streets of downtown New Orleans, dry just hours ago, water was now rising in the midday sun. With my usual space flooded, I parked my car at the Hyatt and waded in rain boots through the two-foot deep water to City Hall.

A number of reporters were hanging out in the hallways. "What do you know?" they asked.

"Not much more than you do right now," I answered frankly.

"How many dead?" came one reporter's query.

"We're not focused on the dead right now," I answered. "There are too many people still needing to be rescued."

"How can you not worry about the dead?" an unseasoned reporter lashed out. I ignored his question.

Local CBS-affiliate anchor Dennis Woltering was standing in the hall. "Dennis, would you like to drive out there and see what we're dealing with?" I asked.

"That would be great," he answered, quickly picking up his tripod.

"Give me a minute," I said.

I entered the emergency center, where the power was now out. Except for the warming temperatures and haggard faces, the room was completely businesslike. Chief Matthews and Colonel Ebbert relayed information to the state homeland security office and FEMA as people hustled in and out. Clusters of relief workers gathered in adjacent rooms while nearby, floors and tables served as makeshift beds.

I looked at the Colonel, whose tousled hair no longer resembled a Marine cut. "I'm trying to get FEMA to set up command and control," he said. "We've gotta move more quickly than we are." I made a mental note to lend more support to the Colonel as calls continued to inundate the emergency center.

"Chief Matthews, you do know people are starting to congregate on the Interstate, right?" I said, doubting that we had contingency plans for this scenario.

"Yes," he said.

Everyone in the room was gathering information, shifting plans and calling for assistance. Floodwaters had inundated police headquarters, the jail, the courts, the evidence room, the armory and all of the police cruisers. Radio antennas were destroyed, but some of the radio channels and land lines continued to operate intermittently. I listened as emergency personnel handled a whirl of calls and sat in the chair next to the babyfaced Captain Mark Willow. Months before, I had worked with Captain. Willow when New Orleans was chosen to host the sixth round of talks for the Central American Free Trade Agreement (CAFTA). He appeared in my office one day and told me he was an undercover officer assigned to monitor people who would come to New Orleans to disrupt the free trade talks.

"These protestors are communicating with each other over the web and are planning to disrupt this event," he warned me then. "Your name is associated with this and they know your address so you need to be very careful."

"Who are these people?" I asked.

"They are the same people who protest at WTO (World Trade Organization) meetings," he answered. "But don't worry – I'm monitoring their blogs and we're on top of this," he assured me. Sitting next to Capt. Willow now, I noticed he did not have the same look of assurance he had shown months earlier.

"How are you, Captain?" I asked.

"Oh God," he said, shaking his head. "People are in their attics and the water is rising up to their neck. We've got police officers getting rescued and then they're jumping back in to rescue other people." He became quiet and I waited while he collected his thoughts. "In over 30 years I have never come close to seeing anything like this. It's beyond words."

"Let me know if you need me to do anything for you," I offered, unsure of what to say. "We'll make it through."

Unlike Capt. Willow, many people would not be able to cope with the disaster. In the coming days, I would notice three distinct types of what I would label "Katrina Madness": zombies, emos and ragers. Zombies would stare into space like ghosts; emos were riddled with anxiety, redirecting all conversation to their personal state of affairs; and ragers displayed incessant anger and bitterness, often at people in power like the Mayor or Governor or President. As I left the emergency center, I hoped very few people with Katrina Madness would wind up in that room.

Walking out through the corridor in City Hall, I grabbed WWL TV's Dennis Woltering and longtime cameraman Tip McClanahan. On Poydras Street, we hopped on board an emergency fire truck in the early afternoon and headed toward Interstate 10. Heading east, we passed the French Quarter, which seemed intact. We soon saw other neighborhoods which had become lakes, getting deeper as we moved from the Tremé district past Bywater and into the Upper and Lower Ninth Wards. Century-old homes and buildings looked like rows of lily pads submerged in water.

As we stopped on the elevated expressway to let Tip shoot B-roll video, I felt a sudden alarm. Several specks moved on the open water. Straining our eyes, we saw people waving for help, many stranded on the highest spot they could find.

"Look over there," said Tip, whose keen photographer's eye caught the slightest movement. A tall, skinny man hung out of a second story window, waving a small cloth over his head. "And over there, too," he pointed further east. Soon we could see white cloths waving on the horizon like lively butterflies in an open field.

"There's another person," said Dennis, pointing to a man on his roof with a yellow shirt waving high above his head. An elderly woman with a blue scarf on her head sat a few feet away from the man, waving too.

"Look at the dogs," I said, as a golden mutt floated by on a small piece of rooftop.

A man stood on the back bumper of an 18-wheeler truck, trying to scramble up the side of the semi as the water rose past his waist. He looked up at us, desperation etched in his hallow face.

Before long, we counted dozens of stranded people and pets in the sea of water. Others gathered on the raised Interstate or stood nervously atop railroad lines, trucks and bridges, filling up any and all dry spaces. Near us, a man with dreadlocks stood over two children dressed only in their underwear.

On the other side of the bridge, a boat carrying a rescued family pulled alongside the highway's railing. As the children began to climb over the rail, Tip positioned his camera on his shoulder to capture the scene. A tense policewoman walked over and pushed him away. A slight tussle ensued as she tried to keep the cameraman from videotaping rescued children.

"What's your name and badge number?" Tip demanded. I could see "Recruit" stamped on the policewoman's shirt.

"None of your business," she answered, emotions frayed by the destruction.

I pulled Tip away. "Come on, let's go."

"I want her reported," Tip said angrily.

"I promise I will pass it on."

Leaving, I noticed a beautiful little boy, about 4 years old, with rosy cheeks and an irresistable smile. I walked over to him.

"Hi," I said. "When the water came, you must have been a brave little boy."

"I was," he said, his scared face lighting up. "I didn't cry once."

"You're stronger than Superman," I said, hugging him tight.

Unbelievably, it would be five horrendous days before many of these survivors would be rescued.

Back at City Hall, I headed out to find the Mayor in the now blazing afternoon heat, believing the busy emergency center could use his help. On the street outside, I ran into my deputy director, TD, as he wiped grubby mud off of his shoes. "Thank goodness you're OK," I said. "Have you seen the Mayor?"

"When I was riding on the Interstate, I could see Big Daddy parked at the heliport," he said.

"Let's get over there," I replied, temporarily forgetting that a small lake now separated us from the heliport. "I really need to talk to him."

The heliport was adjacent to the outside parking lot of the Superdome, but could only be acccessed from the east end of the city. TD and I were determined to get there, even if we had to swim. We searched for transportation that could navigate the floodwaters. As we walked to the almost-flooded intersection of Poydras and Rampart Streets, my borrowed police cap began to attract people urgently in need of help.

"Ma'am, my family can't swim and they're still at home," said a dark-skinned woman in a tattered orange tank top as she ran toward me. "Can you please go get them?"

"Search and rescue teams will pick them up," I said, sickened by her plight.

I moved to a different location to avoid the pleas, but it didn't work. "We need help, please," a voice cried. As I turned around, three women, one adolescent boy and several small children in wet clothes approached me.

"What's wrong?" I asked. Two of the women were crying.

"This is my mother," said the younger of the two, a big-boned girl in her late thirties. "We were at her place and the water just came in so fast."

"We can't find the rest of our family and have nowhere to go," weeped her mother, the deep-set lines near her mouth and eyes now sunburned.

Suddenly a military truck in tan and green camouflauge came driving through the water toward us. "Come with me," I told the women. Several National Guardsmen were perched in the cab, tending to dozens of other rescued residents. "Can you please give us a lift?" I hollered as we waved them down. "We are city officials."

"Yes, but first you'll have to ride with us a few hours to drop these people off on safe ground," answered the guardsman.

We loaded the women and their family members onto the truck, but TD and I had to find a faster way through the water to the heliport. "Thanks anyway," I said.

"Let's try my car," TD said, hoping his SUV could cross the flooded divide. As we walked to his truck, I saw a body lying on the grassy median.

I walked over to the neutral ground and studied the man. "Shit, TD, he's dead." I knew that cold look from when my father passed away.

A woman sat zombie-like next to the corpse. "Can I help you?" I asked, moving closer.

"I carried him all through the water," she said, beginning to cry. "He needed oxygen."

"Ma'am, I'm so sorry," I said. At any other time, someone dying on a downtown street would have elicited immediate support. "TD, we've got to do something about this," I said, hoping he could think of something.

"Let's go," TD prodded. "There's not a thing we can do to help this man."

We quietly got in his car and began to drive. It wasn't long before the car started to take on water. "This isn't going to work," I said. TD brought us back to dry land.

Walking down the street, my police cap brought new cries for help. "Miss, can I talk to you?"

"Yes," I said.

"I'm the general manager of a hotel downtown," said the gray haired man, dressed in a polo shirt and slacks. "We are going to tell our guests to leave the hotel. Where should I direct them?" I knew thousands of people were still in hotels.

"The Dome's surrounded by water, so they would have to be able to swim," I said.

"Where else would you suggest?" he asked, secure in his task, but with a wavering voice of despair for his guests.

"If you have to put them out of the hotel, just have them walk to the Interstate," I assured him. "I'm sure relief will arrive soon." Little did I know that many people would wind up sleeping for days on pavement that was hot enough to fry an egg.

A middle-aged man and a woman both with a small child in their arms walked up to me. "Police, you have to help us," the man said.

"I'm sorry, I was just wearing this cap," I said. I couldn't keep misrepresenting the police force, so I stuck the cap in my purse.

I squinted my eyes in the bright sun and saw TD sprinting down the block toward a white pickup truck stamped with a city seal. Two men were in the cab. I could hardly believe my eyes as TD, who was somewhat of a germaphobe, climbed onto the back of the truck piled high with trash before motioning for me to join him. I ran over, jumped in and immediately smelled the stench.

The driver and his passenger were nervous about driving through the water, which was now almost four feet deep on the street leading to the heliport. As we inched our way closer, the driver screamed out of his window.

"I'm scared, I don't swim, I need to go back!"

"It's OK, just inch forward slowly," I yelled back.

"You can do it," said TD, leaning over the top of the truck to talk to the driver, "just keep moving slowly."

Standing in the bed of the truck on top of the trash, TD and I discussed the worsening conditions. As I breathed through my mouth, without warning the driver threw the truck in reverse and hit the gas pedal.

Suddenly, long, tall TD flew into the slimy trash and I fell right smack next to him. I opened my eyes as I slid deeper into the mountain of filth, finally coming to rest on a greasy McDonald's bag filled with ketchup.

"This is repulsive!" I screamed, looking over at TD.

As we stared at each other in disbelief, we suddenly began to howl, laughing so hard we couldn't stop. "I've never been dirtier in my life," TD laughed, trying to contain his disgust.

The driver made his way out of the flood as we struggled to pull ourselves out of the guck. Finally, we jumped out of the truck, taking time to wipe down as best as possible.

We still had to find an alternate route to the heliport. Soon after we began our search again, a white vehicle screeched to a halt next to me. Denise Estopinal, a public information officer for the Water Board, rolled down her window.

"Sally, it's bad. The pumping stations are going to fail."

"Which ones?" I asked.

"Number 6 and Number 22."

"I will let the Mayor know," I said, trying to remain calm. Pumping station 6 was our most powerful pump and drained not only New Orleans, but also our neighboring region on the west.

"Please inform him quickly," she said. "We have no way of getting through to him." I added one more item to the long list of catastrophes piling up in my mind.

Down the street, we motioned to another National Guard truck. This one was heading to the Dome and would drop us near the heliport. As we rode in the back, the guardsman next to me whistled to his driver to stop.

"What's up?" I asked.

"Look at that guy," he answered, pointing to an elderly man in a wheelchair with water up to his shoulders. "We need to rescue him." Several guardsmen jumped out and waded through the water to carry the man and his wheelchair onto the truck.

The truck brought us to a ramp near the heliport where FEMA was setting up their command base. I was introduced to Phil Parr and some of his FEMA colleagues. Parr, a clean-cut man in his mid 40s, was thoughtful and courteous as he explained FEMA's role in the distribution of food, water, medical supplies and other services. "We want to let the city of New Orleans know that everything is being handled," he assured me.

"So provisions are coming?" I asked, wary since so few resources were in view.

"Yes," he stated emphatically. "We have it under control."

"Good," I said. "We need you big time."

"Bill Lokey is our federal coordinating officer for this disaster, Scott Wells is also here and I am advancing the recovery efforts," Parr said, explaining how FEMA would coordinate its functions with the city and the state. "We are here for your needs." Later I would learn that Parr spent years at the New York Fire Department, and manned the scene of the World Trade Center attack prior to the collapse of the towers.

"Great," I answered. "Let me introduce you to the Mayor if I can find him." We walked over to a landing pad by the heliport and found the Mayor, who had just met with Governor Blanco, Michael Brown, Senator Landrieu and others.

After the introduction, I asked the Mayor about his meeting. "Did you have a successful visit with the delegation that came in?" I asked.

"Yes I did, I told them everything we needed," he said. "I asked the state to hurry and drop sandbags at the 17th Street Canal to stop the flooding."

Late that afternoon, we sat on chairs inside the Entergy command post on the fourth floor of the Hyatt. Because of a small generator the utility company had pre-arranged, lamps dimly lit the room and food trays lined the tables that skirted the walls.

I gave the Mayor his messages, and reiterated the urgent one from Marcia St. Martin. "Don't forget Marcia needs to speak to you," I said. "We've got some pumping stations that are close to failing."

"See if there's any way you can get her on the phone," he instructed. I had several numbers for Marcia – at the safe houses, pumping stations, power plants and home – but I could not get through to her because of broken phone lines. In the early evening, I finally secured a line and handed the Mayor the phone.

"Mr. Mayor," Marcia said urgently, "they never showed up to patch the levee."

"What do you mean?" he asked, cocking his head with a frown.

"No sandbags were dropped," Marcia explained.

"What happened?"

"It is my understanding that the Governor instead sent the choppers to a church in New Orleans East where a thousand people were stranded on the rooftop," she answered.

The Mayor became furious. "She diverted the choppers for a minister?" he said. "A minister had more clout with the Governor than we have? This is a bunch of bull."

I made a note to confirm this story but unfortunately never did.

Police Chief Compass and Marlon the Eagle Scout walked in, now bearing the look of infantry on a battlefield. "One of our guys got shot by a looter," said the Chief, throwing his shirt on the table in disgust. "The officer approached one looter and was shot in the back of the head by a second looter."

Earlier, I had ventured past City Hall to check how far the water was rising. Walking down Canal Street, I saw people taking items from several stores. A man and woman with a small child had apprehensive faces as canned foods teemed out of shopping bags in their hands. In the next block, a younger woman exited a pharmacy carrying a pack of diapers with both arms. But nearly every other person with items in hand had liquor, electronics or an assortment of objects not needed for basic survival. No longer wearing Marlon's police cap, I had turned around to get out of the danger zone.

Upon returning to the Hyatt, I had asked the Mayor, "What about the looting situation?"

"Sally, this is not a priority," he answered. "These people need food."

"Your point's admirable," I had replied, "but there's total lawlessness on Canal Street right now."

Now as Chief Compass and the police manned search and rescue operations, looters were shooting at police officers.

"We need to declare martial law," said the Mayor. A collective sigh engulfed the room.

"Mayor, didn't Sherry say we don't need to declare martial law with the emergency orders we have in place?" I asked him later.

"Double check that with Sherry," he told me. I jotted a note but had no idea how I could get through to Sherry to check on legal matters.

I looked at the Chief. "What else is going on out there?" I asked him.

"You don't want to know," he conceded. "Thugs are just wandering the streets and shooting at us."

"Good God," I replied.

I walked across the hall and saw Paul's worried eyes staring straight ahead as he sat at a table in the Burgundy Room.

"What's up?" I asked.

"I'm worried about my house," Paul said.

"It'll be OK," I said, tapping him on the shoulder.

We worked on messages to disseminate through the reporters down the hall. "We've got gangs of armed men on the streets," Paul said.

"From what the Chief said it sounds like a free-for-all," I replied. "Paul, can you please tell everyone you see to look for Ron? I'm worried sick."

"Sure," he said, gazing ahead.

Late that eveing in the Entergy command post, we secured a dial tone and spoke to Marcia at the Water Board again. "What's up, Marcia?" the Mayor asked into the speakerphone.

"Mr. Mayor, we need immediate action," she replied. "The opening at the 17th Street Canal is a very significant breach. Our plant is flooding."

"What are you telling me?" he asked.

"What this means is that if we don't have support soon and that breach isn't closed, the pumps will fail and the water in the city will be even with the lake," she replied.

"Got it," the Mayor said. "How much time do we have?"

"Only hours," she stated sadly. "Earlier, the water was at our calves and now it's above the thigh, which means it's rising to a dangerously close level with the pumps," she explained. "I have people down there right now watching it. Wait, hold on one second, Mr. Mayor."

We waited on the line while Marcia talked to her engineers.

"This is terrible," she said, coming back on the line. "The engineers just told me the water level is rising too fast. I'm sorry to tell you this, Mr. Mayor, but it's going to happen in 15 or 20 minutes."

"Marcia, what exactly is going to happen in 15 or 20 minutes?" the Mayor asked.

"In 20 minutes or so, we will have no pumping capacity at all. That means within 12-15 hours the city is going to be even with Lake Pontchartrain," she answered softly. "That means St. Charles Avenue will have nine feet of water."

For all of us, but especially for this sturdy woman who had dedicated her whole life to keeping our city dry, this was a devastating blow. How had our levees not held?

We hung up the phone.

"Get the Colonel over here," the Mayor said. Even though I had barely slept and the temperature indoors was nearing 120 degrees, my adrenaline was pumping again.

It was early evening as I crossed the street in the still-deepening water, thankful I could at least touch the ground. "Tell the Colonel we need him now," I relayed to an emergency staffer.

His shoes now scruffy and tidy Marine appearance rumpled, the Colonel left his emergency center post to meet with the Mayor in the Entergy command post. The Colonel could see the fury on the Mayor's face.

"What do you know about the sandbagging efforts?" the Mayor asked the Colonel as he sat at the table.

"First I had been told that a helicopter had dropped sandbags, but then I was told about a problem with the sling on the choppers," the Colonel reported. This was a different story than what Marcia had told us, so we needed to get to the bottom of what had really happened.

"Let's talk to the state," I said, but the Mayor still believed Marcia's story about the ministers.

"This is not right," he charged. "I told them we needed that breach plugged and they made a different call because of politics."

The Colonel sat quietly in his seat twisting his hands together, the Marine insignia gleaming on his ring.

"I don't like this," the Mayor continued. "There are too many freaking cooks in the kitchen."

Facing the Colonel, the Mayor abruptly changed the subject with a surprising directive. "I want to get all of our operations under one roof," he said. "I want to move the entire emergency center operation from City Hall to the Hyatt."

"OK," the Colonel said hesitantly.

When the meeting ended, the Colonel gestured for me to follow him out. "This is a horrible idea," he whispered. "The people in the emergency center have been working their butts off and are doing just fine right where they are. We don't need to disrupt this operation."

"I'll talk to him," I said, but we both knew how stubborn the Mayor could be once he settled on a decision.

"You've got to convince him to change his mind," he said. I wondered how the Marines handled strategy changes, knowing my chances for success were limited.

A few hours later, I delicately approached the subject. "Mayor, do you think it's a good idea to make people move over here right now while they are trying to tend to so many problems?"

"What you need to be thinking about right now is a way to talk to the people in the city, not about our emergency center," he said, saying so much while saying so little.

"Got it," I said.

The Mayor sat stone faced, still peeved at the Governor. "I want to talk to the media about this." We marched down the hall to the room full of reporters.

"I've learned that the plan to drop sandbags into the 17th Street Canal breach didn't happen," the Mayor began. Brett Martel, Erika

Bolstad and Joe Gyan gathered around with their tape recorders and cameras. "As a result, the water has continued to rise and the generators at our pumping stations have shut down. What this means is that soon the entire city will be underwater."

When asked whose fault this was, the Mayor did not mention the Governor but promised to investigate the matter.

"I thought everyone understood this morning that this was the highest priority. The sandbagging was scheduled for midday, but the needed Blackhawk helicopters did not show up," he said. "It didn't get done. Now there's nothing to slow down the pace of the water."

"What does this mean?" one of the reporters asked.

"Soon, the water in the city will be even with Lake Pontchartrain," the Mayor answered. "The bowl is now filling up."

Back in the Entergy command post, the Mayor, Greg the techie and I sat in the stuffy, dimly lit room discussing our inability to communicate with the outside world. Greg was working diligently to restore communications of any kind.

"Scott's got this Vonage internet account that we can use right now," he said, referring to Scott Domke, a member of his team. "With all of this advanced technology, it's some simple internet service that's working for us right now."

"Whatever works, we'll take it," I said.

Chief Compass returned. "We need supplies," he said. "Everything's flooded."

"We can take care of that," the Mayor replied. The Mayor then gave an order to Chief Compass to commandeer whatever he needed to restore order to the city and get looting under control.

"Take whatever you need, just let our guys know they have to follow the law," he told the Chief. "But they can take whatever they need to get the job done."

"OK," said the Chief, his stocky bulk moving toward the door.

"Dude, does this mean me, too?" Greg asked the Mayor.

"Do whatever needs to be done," replied the Mayor.

Greg and the Chief stood at the doorway, discussing what supplies they would need. "Let's hit Office Depot," Greg said.

"Wouldn't this be stealing?" I asked as they laid out their plans.

"Close your ears, Sally," the Mayor responded. "It's getting ugly."

The Chief and Greg left. "Greg, wait," I hollered, running after him. "Put this on your head." I handed over Marlon's police cap. "You might need some protection."

"Thanks, baby," he replied.

"One more thing," I yelled as they walked down the hallway. "We could really use some bullhorns."

Greg and the Chief headed to Office Depot to get technology supplies. Chris Cooper from *The Wall Street Journal* would later capture the story in a front-page article, bringing Greg much notoriety about his role in Mission Impossible.

"Where are the freaking buses?" the Mayor yelled when I walked back into the room.

"The Colonel's working on it and I'm trying to reach the Governor's office," I answered, knowing full well that evacuees in the Dome were becoming scared and restless.

Earlier, the Colonel had told me he was taking this all the way to the White House, demanding to speak to someone high up in the Bush administration. "Where's our help?" he had spewed after receiving word that the USS Bataan, a military ship with full medical facilities, was sitting offshore just waiting for sailing orders. "There's a ship just sitting there!"

"Sally, find Brenda in Baton Rouge and see if she can find the guy from regional transit and get their bus keys," the Mayor instructed.

"OK," I said, both of us unaware that the RTA's buses were now underwater.

"This mess with the sandbags is going to push back our recovery at least another four weeks," the Mayor said. Annoyance with the Governor riddled his face. "We could have drained this city and gotten it all done in eight to ten weeks, but now we're talking three to four months before people can come back in."

Later that evening, the Governor responded on CNN to the Mayor's remarks about the patching of the 17th Street Canal. "The Corps of Engineers has attempted to fix the situation under emergency conditions," Blanco said. Her comments did not address whether helicopters had been diverted.

Deputy Chief Warren Riley came in to update the Mayor. Chief Riley, a reserved but articulate commander, managed day-to-day police operations.

"It's bad out there," he said. "Our officers are screaming over the radio that they're running out of ammunition. That's the first time in my 25 years on the force that I've even heard of a police officer saying he's getting ready to run out of ammo in a gunfight."

I began to feel as if we were living in the Wild Wild West.

"We've got some bad reports coming out of the hotels and hospitals," Chief Riley said. "I'm trying to get officers to each one."

We had also received maydays from inside Touro and Mercy hospitals about dying patients, doctors and nurses ventilating patients manually and drug addicts looting the pharmacies.

"They need to fix their jones," the Mayor said.

"What's that?" I asked.

"When addicts start to go crazy because they haven't had drugs for too long," he said.

"Officers are still performing search and rescue," Chief Riley said, "but we've got to get order on the streets." Composed and professional, Chief Riley now furrowed his brow. "Our biggest problem is we practically have no way to communicate right now."

"Then abandon search and rescue efforts and return to the streets to go after the looters and restore law and order," the Mayor growled.

"We will do that," Riley responded.

"Let's stop this crap now."

The Chief then discussed reports of unrest at the parish jail. "The prison is flooded and some prisoners are out of their cells."

"I know, I received a note from the clerk of court," the Mayor replied. "It's a bad situation there."

"It sounds like there are roughly 30 deputies left to control the situation. They are moving thousands of prisoners onto the Broad Street overpass. I've sent some officers to help them."

"What's up at the Convention Center?" I asked. Earlier in the day, people had begun to gather at the Morial Convention Center since the streets had flooded around the Superdome.

"Conditions are getting worse," Chief Riley answered. "The numbers are growing substantially and people are all over the streets."

"Then open the Convention Center up," said the Mayor.

"OK, but I just want to remind you that there's no way we can check for contraband," he said.

What other choice did we have, I wondered? With 80 percent of the city under water, lifeless bodies floating on the streets, widespread looting, fires burning everywhere, no buses for evacuees, no power in hospitals, no drinking water, gunfire in the air, buildings collapsing and no sanitation for tens of thousands at the Dome, the city was in anarchy. At the height of the pandemonium, a man stood at the uppermost level of the Dome and jumped to his death.

After Chief Riley left, I roamed the hotel. The lack of sanitation was making the environment suffocating and I became lightheaded. Even though it was pitch black outside, I walked out for some fresh air. Gunshots soon rang out so I darted back inside.

Outside the Dome, FEMA's Marty Bahamonde still had Blackberry PIN service. He wrote an e-mail to FEMA Director Michael Brown about evacuees gathering outside the Convention Center. "Estimates [are] that many will die within hours," he wrote. "Sir, I know that you know the situation is past critical."

During the federal investigation, it was revealed that Brown's press secretary replied, "It is very important that time is allowed for Mr. Brown to eat dinner."

Frustrated, Bahamonde vented by Blackberry PIN to another FEMA colleague. "OH MY GOD!!!!!!!! Just tell her [the press secretary] that I just ate an MRE and crapped in the hallway of the Superdome along with 30,000 other close friends so I understand her concern about busy restaurants. Maybe tonight I will have time to move the pebbles on the parking garage floor so they don't stab me in the back while I try to sleep."

Around 10 p.m., a dial tone on one of Entergy's phones gave me the chance to call some local media outlets and CNN, where Aaron Brown spoke to the Mayor. "Mayor, is the city safe tonight?"

"Well, the city is relatively safe considering the circumstances," the Mayor said. "We have probably 80 percent of our city under water, a significant number of residents still in the city, that in these times of the aftermath of the hurricane, they're out looking for food and they started to create some issues with looting."

"Do you have enough law enforcement, whether it's state, local or National Guard to keep control of the city?" Brown asked.

I shook my head no, since we did not have adequate law enforcement and our streets were not safe.

"Absolutely," the Mayor answered.

I studied him closely. It was two and a half days since the storm and the city was not under control, but the Mayor wanted to appear in control. How could we send both messages effectively – we desperately need help, but let's not panic.

"Mayor, this is what we call in my business a hanging curve question. Is there anything else you want to say, you want people to understand about the situation?" Aaron Brown continued.

"The only thing I would point out is everyone knows New Orleans is one of the great, unique cultural cities in the world and we are basically left unprotected right now because of coastal erosion," the Mayor said. "And the big problem we have with this hurricane was there was nothing to subside the tidal surge so coastal erosion is a big challenge going forward."

When the interview ended, I looked at my notes. The word "Buses" was written everywhere. Although we had moved our regional transit buses to higher ground, they still flooded. The yellow buses belonging to the school board had been dealt a similar fate. It was evident now that we should have positioned our bus drivers and buses out of town so they could return once the storm had passed or at least moved the transit buses to even higher ground, like the Interstate or a second floor parking garage.

Sitting silently in the room, Entergy CEO Dan Packer and his number two, Rod West, tried to absorb the news they had overheard earlier about the devastating flooding that would occur. I jotted a note to ask Public Works Director John Shires what type of long-term effects this severe flooding would produce: "John – infrastructure decimated??"

"This is just amazing," said the Mayor. "St. Charles Avenue under nine feet of water."

Robustly built Notre Dame football alum Rod West tried to bring levity to the situation. "Oh, Scarlett," he drawled. "I do declare that my beautiful mansion on St. Charles Avenue is going to be destroyed."

"Now don't you worry, Miss Scarlett," chimed in the Mayor, "we'll help you out of there in no time." I chided them to stop while I smiled at the brief reprieve.

I finally reached the Governor's office before midnight. Andy Kopplin, the Governor's smart, levelheaded chief of staff, informed us that Guard troops were being mobilized to assist us.

"Andy, please hear me — we really need buses right now," I stressed. "There are a lot of problems but we need you to just work on getting the people out of this city. We need the buses."

"I've got it," he said. "Let me tell you what we're doing for the buses. We were counting on FEMA buses, but we've also put out a massive alert to schools throughout the state for buses and bus drivers in case FEMA doesn't come through." Agitation about the lack of response was now bleeding through almost every discussion.

"Andy, just for clarification, can you repeat what we need?" I asked.

"Buses are the number one priority," he said. I thanked him as the Mayor listened, hoping Andy would properly convey the message to everyone at the state.

In the wee hours of the morning, I walked from floor to floor to find a room that didn't smell and wound up back in the room that Ron and I had originally been given on the 24th floor. I opened the closet and shined my flashlight into my suitcase, discovering a small grocery bag with Ritz Bits crackers, a bottle of water and, as luck would have it, my vitamins. In 1992, I had been diagnosed with a malignant melanoma and needed daily antioxidants to ward off the return of cancer. In this battle for our city, I was not about to let the ugly C-word come creeping back in.

I lay on the bed, realizing it had to be three or four in the morning. Worried about Ron, I became sick to my stomach.

Chapter 6

Waving the White Flag

Wednesday, August 31

I woke up wondering where I was. My body was filthy and for reasons I couldn't comprehend my muscles ached. The hotel curtains flapped in the broken window, reminding me of the nightmare I was living.

Staggering down to the nearly deserted fourth floor, I peeked in on the reporters' corner room. A putrid smell rose from the dirty socks strewn along the floor. Seeing no one, I headed to the stairwell and took a deep breath before opening the door. Hotel guests were now using any semi-private area in the luxury hotel as a bathroom. I worked hard not to step in the excrement as I flew up the stairs to the Mayor's suite on the 27th floor, dirty socks now more reminiscent of perfume.

"Anything new?" I asked as I entered his more orderly suite.

"Someone was shot at the Dome last night," he said, his hand cranking a wind-up transistor radio. "It was either a policeman or National Guardsman."

"What's the status on the injury, for Heaven's sake?" I asked.

"I'm waiting for word," he said.

I sat on his floor and jotted down notes. "I saw Doc Stephens," I said, changing the subject.

"How's the medical team holding up?" he asked.

"Fine," I answered, "but Doc says we can't walk through the water anymore because we could easily pick up staph infection." Doc had fussed when I told him I had to go through the water several times a day.

"These infections can be life threatening, Sally," he'd said.

"But how will I get to City Hall?" I had asked the doctor.

"I don't know," he answered. "Maybe you just shouldn't go." I hoped I didn't already have a disease. I was wading regularly through the muckity muck and at one point passed quite close to a floating body.

As I marked down updates, the Mayor was becoming more and more agitated with what he saw as the state's lack of urgency in getting the buses into the city. "Where are the freaking buses?" he repeated.

"They should be here soon," I said unconvincingly.

Although the Interstate was flooded from the West, a clear transportation path existed via the Crescent City Connection right into downtown New Orleans. Earlier, a police officer told me that the lack of buses was the result of drivers afraid of the security risk within the city. "These drivers aren't willing to lose their lives," the officer had said. Whatever the reason, it was clear buses were not making their way into the city.

"Mayor, I've tried to get messages to Brenda to see if she could track down keys to the RTA buses, but I'm told the area that they parked the buses is under water," I said.

"It is," the Mayor confirmed.

In the adjoining room, bodyguard Wondell had awakened and found a dial tone after picking up his phone. We pulled the phone into the den and I called our press secretary, Tami, who was now in Houston.

"'Good Morning America' would like to talk to the Mayor," she said. "Let me see if I can patch you through."

Charlie Gibson came on the line. "Mayor, can you hear me?"

"Charlie, I can hear you just fine," the Mayor replied.

"I'm not quite clear on how much water you're getting in the city right now," he said.

"As a matter of fact, I'm on the 27th floor of a very un-air conditioned building looking out over the city, and where there was dry land, there is now several feet of water. So, what's happening right now is the bowl effect that everybody talked about is happening as we speak. And the water will rise to try and equal the water level of the lake, which is three feet above sea level. And that's significant because on St. Charles Avenue, one of our most famous avenues, it's six feet below sea level in elevation. So, there will be nine feet in that area and probably 20 feet in other areas of the city."

After the interview, we received a report on the water levels in the city. The tide in Lake Pontchartrain had begun to fall, perhaps due to water flowing out of some of the other levee breaches. This welcomed news meant that the flooding might not get as high as we had expected.

"Are you up for another interview?" I asked the Mayor.

"Let's do it," he replied. I called the "Today" show.

"Mr. Mayor, good morning to you," said Natalie Morales. "At first people said that it appeared that New Orleans had dodged a bullet. How dire is the situation there?"

"The city is under a significant amount of water, and we have a breach that I'm now getting reports that we may have closed and the water may have stabilized, but we still have a pretty dire situation with water in at least 80 percent of the city," he said.

We wrapped up the interviews and headed to the Dome. Piercing sunrays filled the stagnant air.

"This ain't right, Mayor Nagin," yelled a short and stocky man in a blue T-shirt as we worked our way through the crowds gathered on the ramp. The hair on his arms was sticky and his body was covered in sweat. "You can't leave us like this." Buses were nowhere in sight.

"We don't deserve to be treated like this," said a woman in a flimsy pink cotton dress as she approached me. "It's hot, there's no electricity and we have no place to go to the bathroom."

"I'm so sorry," I said, hugging the bones protruding from her back.

The Mayor was consoling another frail woman nearby. "Hang in there, sweetheart," he said. Because of the unsavory conditions in the Dome, evacuees were beginning to resemble a war-torn population.

"These are my people," Hyatt security chief and Ninth Ward native Gralen Banks later told me, "and even I don't recognize them anymore."

Makeshift cardboard beds lined the ramp. "How long can they sleep on the ground like this?" I asked.

A National Guardsman assigned to maintaining order walked next to us. "We're sleeping on the ground, too," he told me. "We feel their pain."

"You're all heroes," I replied, embarrassed that members of the Guard were also in such a deplorable environment.

"Thanks."

"How's the temperature of the crowd?" I asked. "And are you seeing any problems?"

"What you would expect," he answered. "There are some drugs and booze, but the biggest problem is the heat and overflowing toilets. People are going to the bathroom in the hallways."

"We've got the same thing at the Hyatt," I said. As we talked, I gazed at the crystal clear sky and realized how easily choppers could lower port-o-lets onto the ramp.

We walked away as evacuees shouted at the Mayor to return. At the FEMA staging area, Phil Parr introduced us to Scott Wells, FEMA's Federal Coordinating Officer for Louisiana. With white hair and soft blue eyes, Wells displayed an accommodating nature.

I observed what appeared to be a satellite phone station and ran toward it. "We urgently need to use these phones," I told the guardsman. "Our satellite phones are dead and our landlines are hardly working." With breaks in the cable network that made up the backbone of service for the local telephone company, dial tones were practically nonexistent, particularly when a phone needed electricity to work.

"These phones aren't working either, I'm afraid," he told me. Satellite phones were meant to be the most secure line of communication during emergencies.

"Why don't your sat phones work?" I screamed as respectfully as possible while a chopper whipped overhead.

"We're not sure," the guardsman replied.

"Let's try anyway," I said. He helped, but the call did not go through.

"This is scary," I told him. "Emergency phones of all kinds and at all levels incapable of working."

"Sally?" said an unfamiliar voice as I left the satellite station. I turned to see Dr. Fred Cerise, a grammar school classmate whom I had seen only once during the past 30 years and who was now Louisiana's secretary of health and hospitals.

"Fred," I said, "It's so great to see you." We hugged, knowing the emotions we felt came from more than just the meeting of two old friends. Fred had set up a MASH-style unit in the raised parking lot between the heliport and the Dome ramp.

"How are they?" I asked.

"They're mostly dehydrated," he said, his sleep-deprived eyes scanning patients on every cot in the tents. "But we do have some really sick people that we're trying to stabilize so they can get airlifted out of here." The number of special needs patients, 500 when the Dome first opened, had now grown substantially. Fred wore a firm resolve to save each patient as we bid each other goodbye.

Moving across the makeshift medical unit, we spoke to Brigadier General Brod Veillon of the Louisiana National Guard. General Veillon had moved from the flooded Jackson Barracks to the Superdome and was helping to direct transport operations.

National Guard Sergeant Anthony Dazet moved us to a waiting chopper so we could again survey the city. "I'm here to help with anything you might need," he said, as helicopters landed on the nearby loading zone in the blazing morning sun.

As we lifted off, the city swept into view like a soup bowl filled to the brim. After a few minutes in the air, messages appeared on rooftops spelling out HELP. Many homes had moved off their foundations and floated into nearby neighborhoods. Broken gas lines caused fires to erupt along the surface of the water.

So many distinct characteristics of New Orleans were nowhere to be seen, including our elaborate cemeteries, built above the ground in a city below sea level. As the propellers whirled, the Mayor grabbed my notebook and wrote, "Future quote: For a city that buries its deceased above ground, even the dead drowned."

At the levee breach near the 17th Street Canal in Lakeview, a lone man stood barefoot in shorts on a rooftop. Fear flooded his face. The pilot circled over him, alerting the survivor that he had been seen (and would soon be rescued, I hoped).

We headed east, where it looked like thousands of people were still stranded. In one neighborhood, a middle aged man held onto a piece of wood, waving feverishly toward us. The pilot hovered overhead and dropped provisions into the darkened water nearby. The man held onto the splintered plywood and kicked quickly toward the package.

Flying east to Slidell, the Interstate over Lake Pontchartrain resembled a set of dominoes that had been knocked down with the flick of a thumb as the wildly tossed concrete slabs exposed the power of the storm's surge.

We flew over the outskirts of neighboring St. Bernard Parish before heading toward the Ninth Ward. As we hovered above the large breach in the Industrial Canal floodwall, the Mayor pointed out a barge that had floated into the flooded neighborhood.

We landed back at the heliport and spotted a small, lost dog. "Look at this precious black puppy," I said. "It looks like a shih tzu."

The Mayor picked up the dog and held it close in his arms.

In the heliport's reception area, FEMA's Scott Wells and Phil Parr, the National Guard's General Landreneau and Brigadier General Veillon, Colonel Ebbert, the Mayor and I waited. A lone Coast Guard pilot dressed in a green khaki uniform and orange vest paced nearby.

As we mingled in the crowded room, we received word that a chopper carrying the President's new appointee to the hurricane recovery had landed. "The President has named General Russell Honoré head of Joint Task Force Katrina to coordinate active-duty support for disaster relief," Scott Wells informed us.

A half-chewed cigar in his mouth, General Honoré swaggered in wearing bulky military boots, army fatigues and a dark beret that hovered over a George Patton look of confidence on his face. As introductions were made, we congregated around this leader of the 82nd Airborne, 1st Cavalry, 1st and 2nd Marine Expeditionary Forces. Exuding the charm and magnetism of a Southerner, Honoré vigorously shook hands with those gathered tightly around to meet the President's new appointee. Soon, we formed a small circle in the few chairs inside the heliport's tiny meeting space.

The Mayor opened the meeting by recounting the significant destruction that had thus far occurred. "General, let me tell you where we are. We've got water everywhere except on our West Bank. Search and rescue operations are going on all over the city, but fires and looting are causing additional problems."

Phil Parr gave an operational update from FEMA. "FEMA is here to head up command and control," Parr said, laying out the work of his emergency response teams.

Colonel Ebbert presented challenges from the emergency center. "We've been trying to get the help we need, but it's not coming fast enough."

Impatiently, a Coast Guard pilot interrupted the meeting. "I've got a whole field of choppers ready to go and I just need the order to fly." He was ignored as the conversation drifted back to recovery.

"Search and rescue is continuing," said General Landreneau. "The State Wildlife and Fisheries office has had hundreds of boats in the water since the storm cleared out."

"We need to make sure we follow FEMA guidelines in how we do everything," Parr interrupted. His words thudded down like sandbags as he rattled off technicalities that made me wonder if FEMA's motto was "just say no."

Scott Wells interrupted when he noticed that the rules and regulations were not of grave concern to the small group gathered in the room. "We're going to see this operation through," he said optimistically.

"Please listen everyone!" General Veillon suddenly shouted over the voices reverberating over Parr's. He pulled a white handkerchief from his pocket and emotionally waved it over his head as a flag of surrender. "We have 25,000 people in the Dome with no power, extreme heat and no bathrooms." He now had the attention of everyone in the room.

"This is a dangerous situation and I'm about to wave our flag in defeat!" he cried. Desperate for someone to chart a different course, General Veillon stared hard at each of us.

Parr answered, but again began to talk about FEMA's rules and regulations, clearly the last thing we needed in the throes of this emergency. I was beginning to think that FEMA would instruct us to stand our ground in a pedestrian crosswalk as a fast moving 18-wheeler bore down just because the rule said we had the right to be there. We would be right, but dead right.

Exasperated, General Honoré spoke for the first time, interrupting Parr. "Excuse me, FEMA, but I think before you say another word, you need some fucking successes."

Ouch. No bureaucratic double-talk from this general, I felt like cheering. Finally someone had arrived who could toss out the broken record, stop the bleeding and turn this into a can-do operation. I felt bad for Parr, but I knew tough words were needed to challenge his years of FEMA indoctrination.

Honoré took the floor and immediately commanded each participant into task mode. It was clear to everyone a new sheriff was in town.

The Coast Guard pilot who had been frantically trying to talk was finally given the floor. "I have 35 choppers just waiting to go," he shouted. "We're sitting there waiting for the order. We can easily fly in and out of this heliport. I just need the order."

"You've got the order," commanded General Honoré. "Go fly."

I looked at the Mayor. He smiled. General Honoré was now our gutsy commander. We hoped the cavalry was close behind.

I walked outside the heliport and sat on the curb of the landing pad to write the kids a note. It had been two days since I had seen or heard from Ron and I missed my family dearly. I was sure he was in the city, but where, and was he OK? I sat down and jotted an e-mail to the kids even though they would not receive it.

"Hi my beautiful children," I wrote. "I just had to tell you how much I love you and miss you. This is such a difficult time – the city is devastated. I just finished a meeting with the General that's been sent to take this operation over."

I wondered how much I could open the floodgates and remembered they wouldn't get the e-mail. "By the hour, more people are dying from no water, no food and drowning. I am sorry to be so graphic, but this whole situation is the saddest thing you can ever imagine," I said. "All I want to do is hug the 2 of you and Dad. I will be there very soon to pick you up and figure out where we go from here." I signed it, "Hugs and love, kisses and misses, Mom."

As we made our way back through the crowds at the Dome, once again the throngs approached. As people gathered around the Mayor, a light-skinned woman with an infant in her arms walked over to me. "We're not going to survive," she said.

I gave her the best encouragement I could muster. "You're going to make it and so is your beautiful baby."

"We need to be able to speak to them, Sally," the Mayor said sternly as we exited.

"I know, I've got Greg and the police trying to commandeer bullhorns," I said. "I've also talked to the Coast Guard to see if they have bullhorns on their choppers." I had also tried to find someone who could take my flyer to Baton Rouge and make copies, but no one that I spoke to was leaving.

The Mayor looked piercingly at me as if my efforts were inadequate.

"I'm sorry, Mayor," I said, drastically looking for a workable solution. "We can put you inside the Dome and have you shout to small groups but their PA system is no longer working."

"I'm not going to shout to small groups," he said.

When we arrived back at the Hyatt, employees from our emergency center in City Hall lined the fourth floor halls as the move to the City Hall was initiated. "Any way to stop this stupid move?" someone seethed.

"Not yet," I answered.

Back in our makeshift bunker, we received more reports of looting. "They are stealing electronics, clothes, jewelry, all kinds of stuff," Marlon said, his Eagle Scout nature now menacing. "They're stealing guns, too," he added in disgust, "which is very different than taking food because you're hungry."

Earlier, we had taken a ride down Canal Street and witnessed a crowd pushing on the glass doors of an Asian restaurant. "We need food," the crowd screamed.

The frightened owners stood inside and shouted, "We have nothing." Police officers, no longer intervening, had walked right by. I was sure by now the crowd had broken into the restaurant.

"Where's the additional troops that were supposed to have arrived by now?" the Mayor demanded in the Entergy command post.

"And where's the Red Cross?" I added.

No one answered because no one knew.

I walked downstairs to go to City Hall. Leaving the Hyatt, I said hello to a police officer who had been manning one of the checkpoints at the entrance to the hotel. I recognized him from the previous days.

"I'll bet you can help me," he said. "You work with the Mayor, right?"

"Yes."

"I need to ask you something personal."

"Go right ahead," I replied.

"Can you please get me some anti-depressants? I've been off of my meds now for days and so have some of the other guys." He had a hint of urgency in his eyes.

"What kind do you need?" I asked.

"Paxil, Proloft, Prozac – whatever you can get your hands on."

"I'll do it," I told him, hoping that the outcome of this assignment would be more successful than patching the breaches, finding bullhorns or securing buses.

I walked to City Hall to find Chief Parent, ignoring Doc's plea to stay out of the water. A huge fire of unknown origin was burning on the West Bank of New Orleans, across the Mississippi River, and I needed to see what Chief Parent knew about the fire.

A message from Audrey arrived. "Ann Macdonald is trapped in a home on Gentilly Blvd., running out of power and water, and Tenaj's fiancé is trapped with others in Southern University's auditorium." Ann and Tenaj were our colleagues at City Hall so I brought the message to Chief Matthews in the emergency center.

Inside, first responders stood around the table, reacting to emergency messages being brought to them from people throughout the city. Watching the constant flow of work made me realize how irresponsible it was to be moving this team in the middle of a crisis. I made a note to talk to the Mayor again.

Back at the Hyatt, I caught up with the Mayor. A reporter shouted a question as we passed by. "Mayor, how many people have died?" It was becoming an all too familiar question.

"Minimum, hundreds. Most likely, thousands," said the Mayor.

"Where did you get that number?" I asked him later.

"Do the math, Sally," he answered. "If we had 80 percent of the population leave, that leaves 100,000 people still here. We've got 35,000 at the Dome and 15,000 at the Convention Center, that's 50,000 unaccounted for. What do you think? One percent, five percent perished?" We would later learn that even more than 80 percent had evacuated, accounting for an even smaller death toll than originally feared.

At the table in the Entergy command post, the phone rang. "Hello?" I answered, surprised but delighted that the phone had rung.

"Hi, who is this?" said a woman's voice.

"Sally Forman with the City of New Orleans," I answered.

"Just who I need to speak to," she said.

"Good, how can I help you?" I asked.

"This is Kim Martin. We have just left Kindred Hospital on Prytania Street by boat." Doc Stephens had told me about this small hospital, but I still couldn't place its location.

"I need you to get word to Doc Stephens," she continued. "He needs to tell whomever is coming to this hospital after us that when they walk in, dead bodies will be right in front by the door. We left the bodies right there and I don't want anyone to be surprised by it."

"Got it, thanks," I said. I made a note in a column I had titled "The Dead."

The Colonel came to the Hyatt. Already short-fused, he had hardly slept since the storm hit and was fed up with Washington's lack of support. "I spoke to the White House this morning and I let them know what I was thinking," he said, his respect for chain of command diminishing each hour help did not arrive.

"Who was on the phone?" I asked.

"Josh Fuller, who works for Secretary Chertoff, and some other people were in the room," he said.

"What happened?" the Mayor asked.

"I told them that we need troops to establish our organizational capabilities and to help our police who are under attack," he said, his voice rising. "I told them, 'we have no command and control, no communications, no troops and FEMA is pretty much non-existent' so that they could hear it directly from me."

I looked at the Colonel, his dapper style now replaced with piercing eyes and dirty black hair.

"You know what else?" he said, his steely eyes looking at me, "I told them that we have received no federal support and that we are watching the city die. I don't think they liked that. There was a general in the room who was so mad he left," he said.

"Good for you, Colonel," I said. Getting this off of his chest seemed to make the situation more bearable.

"He should come down here and work next to you," I said, "then let's see how he feels."

Someone handed me a note. I opened it. It was from Ron. "Sally, keep up the good work. I'm going between the zoo and aquarium. Tried to get to you last night, but there was too much water. Love, Ron."

"Thank God he's alive," I shouted.

That afternoon, the President held a press conference with his cabinet and outlined plans to deliver equipment and provisions to the Gulf Coast. *The New York Times* criticized it in an editorial:

Waiting for a Leader

George W. Bush gave one of the worst speeches of his life yesterday, especially given the level of national distress and the need for words of consolation and wisdom. In what seems to be a ritual in this administration, the president appeared a day later than he was needed. He then read an address of a quality more appropriate for an Arbor Day celebration: a long laundry list of pounds of ice, generators and blankets delivered to the stricken Gulf Coast. He advised the public that anybody who wanted to help should send cash, grinned, and promised that everything would work out in the end.

Greg the techie walked in. "Here, I'm now your secretary," he said sarcastically, handing me a note.

"I know the feeling well," I said.

The note said that the President was trying to get in touch with the Mayor. It had been relayed to us earlier that the President had visited New Orleans. "He flew over in Air Force One."

When we were alone, the Mayor commented that it "must have been one serious telescope to observe the city from a 747."

"That's not a visit," I said. The people at the Dome and on rooftops must have looked like ants.

We needed to reach the President on Air Force One. This would be interesting – sat phones weren't working and we couldn't easily talk to our colleagues and families, so how on earth were we going to reach Air Force One? I attempted anyway by asking National Guardsmen if their satellite phones were working, checking the lines in the Entergy command post and talking to police to see if the radios were functioning. Several hours later, Greg the techie secured a line for us on a new set of telephones he had "commandeered" for the team.

"Yeah, baby," Greg said in his Austin Powers voice as he handed over a blaring dial tone. We laughed at the humor that rivaled his determination to help the city communicate.

The Mayor spoke first to Andrew Card, White House Chief of Staff. Card assured the Mayor that the Department of Homeland Security was sending equipment and people to the city, including security forces. We hoped that meant the cavalry was finally on its way.

When the Mayor finally spoke to the President, he asked for help. "Mr. President, I need the levees at the 17th Street Canal patched. Our pumping stations are destroyed and we need attention brought there immediately."

"We'll take care of that," said the President.

They talked for a moment about search and rescue and exchanged pleasantries. When they hung up, I asked the Mayor why he didn't ask for more.

"Let's get him to do one job and do it right and then we'll ask for the next thing," he said, demonstrating his methodical nature.

After the call, the Mayor and I analyzed the most pressing problems, including the buses. "Houston is preparing to take evacuees into the Astrodome," I said.

"First the buses have to get here," he answered.

The other shoe fell when a report from the emergency center said our buses were being stopped at the clover leaf Interstate ramps in Metairie to pick up evacuees who had been dropped off there. A suburb of New Orleans, Metairie stayed mostly high and dry.

The Mayor went berserk. "This is b.s. and I'm not going to let this happen again," he fumed. "All the Governor has to say is, 'don't let those buses stop 'til they get to New Orleans.'"

I wondered if anyone really knew how bad the situation was. Inside the Dome, a fire had erupted. The streets were chaotic and dangerous. People were still drowning and hungry. If they couldn't send buses, couldn't choppers with slings just pick people up? Were safety concerns still keeping cars from entering the city to pick people up at the Convention Center? Couldn't someone just dump water or ice to desperate citizens on the Interstate?

Weeks after the storm, when one of several new cell phones I was carrying rang, I picked up the unfamiliar device. "Hello."

"Hi Sally, this is Donald Trump Jr." he said. "We own an ice company and can send in several planes of ice if you need it."

Later, I would think about all of the help like this that probably tried to get in the first week after the storm but somehow couldn't and therefore hadn't. How precious ice would have been to the people on the blistering highways and in the suffocating Dome.

I finished the evening as I did every other, canvassing the fourth floor of the Hyatt from the Entergy command post, to the Burgundy Room where we had some small food trays and snacks that I could nibble, then down to the media room at the end of the hall. I peeked in on the reporters as they pounded away on their laptops, seemingly oblivious to the worsening smell of dirty socks. I scanned the thousands of Hyatt guests still holed up in the third floor ballroom, confined to cramped quarters, which could easily produce another Dome-like situation. I made a note to check with the general manager to see how the guests were holding up.

After I performed a final check on the ground level, an overhead light near the front desk attracted me. I had written down important notes but needed light to organize them. I pulled out all of my papers to determine the top priorities for the morning. The clock on the wall read 1:40 a.m. right before the scream.

"You!" shouted a hotel security officer running through the outside garage door right over to me. "Just who I need!" I recognized the man as one of the Hyatt's security officers. "We figured out a way to get a provision truck in for the people still here at the hotel. Now looters have surrounded it and they're stealing the food." His voice conveyed a mixture of fear and fury.

"Dang it to hell," I murmured under my breath.

"The security we hired to convoy the truck just took off," he said. "The truck is still nowhere near the hotel."

"Wait here," I told him. "Let me grab Chief Compass." I bolted up four flights of stairs and ran to the room where the Chief and his deputies were sleeping, realizing that safety threats could destroy our ability to receive resources. "Marlon, wake up," I said, arriving at his cot first. He woke up quickly.

"Eddie, wake up," I said as I shook the arm of the Police Chief. Neither of them had gotten much sleep in days.

"What, what?" he asked as he bounced up.

"There's a problem downstairs with a provision truck trying to get into the city."

"Everybody up," the Chief hollered to all of his brass in the room. "We need help downstairs." We all ran back down the stairs together as I filled them in on what I knew.

Downstairs, the Chief told the Hyatt's security director he needed use of the hotel's emergency PA system. Suddenly the Chief's voice was broadcast into all of the hotel rooms.

"This is Police Chief Eddie Compass," he said. "I need all able-bodied men and women in this hotel to come down to the first floor, that's level one."

Chief Compass, Marlon and a handful of other officers ran out of the hotel to circle the truck, still blocks away from the Hyatt. Inside the hotel, people came downstairs in droves, seeming to sense a need much greater than sleep. From the ground floor, hundreds of people held hands and formed a human chain to deliver the goods to the third floor of the hotel. From one hand to another, cereal boxes, flashlights, water and milk flowed in.

Once the chaos ended, I looked for a place to sleep. The rooms with blown out windows were the coolest. All I had to do was flip the mattress and keep my shoes on to protect my feet from shattered glass. Gentlemen that they were, Louis and Wondell would sometimes help me, even checking the bathroom to make sure it had not yet been used.

That night, Secretary Chertoff issued a press release. "We are extremely pleased with the response that every element of the federal government, all of our federal partners, have made to this terrible tragedy."

Had I read it, I would have become ill. Here we were sitting in a war zone. Disease, death and violence surrounded us. The Governor was telling us that soldiers and buses were coming, but we saw none of it. The President had said the cavalry was coming, but we didn't see them. Hell, we hadn't even seen any of their scouts.

Chapter 7

A National Disgrace

Thursday, September 1

I woke up and treaded carefully around shards of glass. As I looked in the mirror attached to the closet door, I saw that my thick head of hair had begun to resemble a rat's nest. Since I colored my hair, I checked my budding roots. No longer in possession of Marlon's protective police cap, I was thrilled to find my son McClain's University of Texas baseball cap in the closet. Ignoring the rank smell of the clothes I had now been wearing for several days, I placed the cap on my head and sauntered out.

I walked through the Hyatt to the third floor plaza breezeway that was connected to the Dome's outer ramps. Large crowds of people stood shoulder to shoulder jammed against the glass doors as National Guardsmen kept order with barricades. A few buses had pulled up, but with crowds like this, hundreds more would be needed.

I went downstairs and stepped outside. In the fetid water, floating debris was now more visible. What in the hell is this stuff, I wondered.

To quell my panic, I gazed up. Smoke and helicopters splintered the skyline.

Inside the emergency center, tempers were beginning to flare. "This is an incredibly explosive situation we've got," the Colonel said, his once strong military posture now hunched over in near defeat. "We can send massive amounts of aid to tsunami victims but can't bail out the city of New Orleans."

How could we get to a better place, I wondered? Looking back, I should have stayed in the emergency center, taken the time to think about the answer to this fundamental question and made more strategic decisions. Instead, I walked back to the Hyatt and stayed busy responding to every crisis coming my way.

The Mayor was in the Entergy command post.

"See if you can reach the executive staff," he said. After several attempts on Entergy's speakerphone, I reached Brenda in Baton Rouge.

"Brenda, I have the Mayor with me," I said. "We're OK and checking in."

"We're fine, too," she replied, her collected demeanor reassuring us. "Everyone is here and we've been getting a lot of work done."

"Good," I said. The Mayor listened quietly.

"In fact," Brenda continued, "we are moving forward with a contract to clean up the city." The Mayor listened closely. "We have talked to different companies that have environmental clean-up experience and we've decided on the Shaw Group," Brenda said. "In fact, we are moving into their offices in Baton Rouge and will operate out of there."

The Shaw Group, one of Louisiana's only Fortune 500 companies, was an environmental clean-up company based in Baton Rouge. What Brenda did not know was that we had been told that The Shaw Group diverted a supply ship on its way to New Orleans for Shaw's own purposes. Based on this rumor and the fact that Jim Bernhard, CEO of the Shaw Group, was a major donor to the Governor, the Mayor didn't trust the company.

"Brenda, slow down," the Mayor said into the speakerphone as he shook his head. "Cancel whatever you have with The Shaw Group. Every vulture in America is going to be circling right now."

"OK," said Brenda, somewhat taken aback by the directive, but still willing to follow orders.

I relayed instructions on items we needed the team to accomplish from Baton Rouge. Looking back, I know that our team worked hard, but the overall lack of cooordination showed we didn't work smart.

When we hung up, the Mayor instructed me on how we would proceed. "Sally, we have to remember that unless someone is here in New Orleans and can see firsthand what we are dealing with, they have no idea what is happening. Those people are operating in a pre-Katina mode, doing things based on politics," he said. "They're not calling any shots, we're going to be making all the decisions from here."

"OK," I said.

Chief Compass came into the room. "There are people with guns inside the Convention Center," he said. The situation had worsened with estimates of 20,000 people gathered there with no food or water on hand.

"What's going on?" the Mayor asked.

"I almost got kidnapped inside," he said. "We were trying to calm the crowd and they tried to take me as a hostage."

I stood up as he removed his shirt, dripping with sweat. The Chief and his officers had now been on the streets in open combat for several days.

"It's dark inside the Convention Center. People are shooting at officers, but we can't shoot back because we don't want to hit innocent people," he moaned.

"Who was there with you?" I asked.

"The state police abandoned our officers there. We were left there alone to fend for ourselves." We had little reason not to believe his every word.

"I'm going to tell the people who are there to march," roared the Mayor. "If they can't get the buses to us, let's get the people to the buses."

"Great idea," I told him as I drafted a statement. People who were worried their last refuge might flood needed to know that they could escape by walking to the Interstate and crossing the brige

"Maybe people will have to walk all the way to LaPlace, but at least they can get picked up there," the Mayor added.

"If I was stranded with no food and water, I would walk 'til I dropped," I said. The Mayor and I drafted the statement. "Let's title it 'WALK,'" I said.

"This is a desperate SOS," he said. "Right now we are out of resources at the Convention Center and don't anticipate enough buses. We need buses. Currently the Convention Center is unsanitary and unsafe and we're running out of supplies."

I walked down to find the reporters inside the Hyatt. I had still not seen any local radio reporters who could broadcast messages to evacuees with transistor radios.

A little later in the Entergy command post, I looked up as General Honoré, in his olive green and khaki uniform, entered the room and sat at the table across from the Mayor. The General's aides, wearing maroon berets and similar uniforms, sat in chairs along the wall of the dimly lit room. Scott Trahan, the General's levelheaded aide-de-camp, sat next to him.

Scott took meticulous notes for the General and was adept at producing his cigar at the perfect moment. The General, a man of few words, would turn to the aide, grunt a command, and turn back around.

"Yes, sir, whatever you say, sir," Scott would tell the General.

I realized my current job was more aide-de-camp to the Mayor and right now, I too could also use an aide-de-camp.

"Mr. Mayor," General Honoré said with the cigar in his mouth. "We know there are challenges and we are on top of them but Katrina was a biblical-type event." The Mayor listened intently. "Sir, what do you see as the priorities moving forward?" General Honoré asked respectfully. The General was a Creole from Louisiana who could understand not only the situation on the ground, but also the culture of our people.

The Mayor answered methodically. "Priority number one is evacuating the sick people both in the Dome and in our hospitals, number two is search and rescue and number three is securing the buses, which the state tells me they are doing but I haven't seen that yet."

General Honoré paid close attention, like Sun Tzu on the battlefield, getting to know the enemy as well as he knew himself.

"I'm also working on patching the levees and securing our streets," the Mayor concluded. "These are the top priorities right now."

"Is there anything else?" he asked.

I quickly interjected. "General, the Police Department is badly in need of ammunition and other critical items. Do you think you could help with that?"

"Read me what you've got," he said. His aide took careful notes.

"We need 400 M-4's with 25,000 5.56 caliber rounds," I said. Even though my father had been a military policeman, I had no idea what an

M-4 even was. Earlier, when Chief Riley had given me his list of needs, he had to repeat the ammunition requirements twice since I had such little knowledge of weapons.

"Three hundred vests," I continued, "we need fuel sent to 4800 General Meyer on the West Bank, 1,500 military boots, 1,000 handcuffs, and 200 cars – Crown Vics if possible." The police had been wiped out of everything, including cars, weapons, equipment, radios and clothes. "That's not all," I said. "If you can, please add 200 laptop computers and 200 handheld police computers."

"Take care of that," Honoré told his trusted aide.

By the time resources began to flow to the Police Department, the city was virtually empty.

As we wound down the meeting, I was feeling more hopeful. I looked up and saw Ron.

"Where on earth have you been?" I said, running to embrace him. We moved to a hallway behind the Entergy command post. A set of portable steps sat perched in a storage room and we settled on them to talk.

"I've mainly been at the aquarium," he said, "but we could see the water moving toward it on Canal Street so I told the staff there that it was time to leave."

"Are you safe there?" I asked.

"It was awkward being alone, so I went out to look for help from the police."

"Any luck?" I asked.

"I finally found a police sergeant on Canal Street and told him I had a dry and secure building," he said. "He told me as long as I could take the entire communications unit from the 6th District, they would move to the aquarium."

"So they're there?"

"Yep, and they've been great."

"How are the animals?"

"The generators are shutting down now," he said. "We've lost over a thousand fish so far but the police are helping me feed the ones that are still alive."

"Good for them," I said. "What are their names so I can let the Chief know?"

"I'll get them for you," he said. We hugged each other tightly.

"I'm going to have to go back out to get fuel for the aquarium," Ron said.

"I don't think any trucks are getting through," I said. "We haven't seen one bus."

"I have to try," he said. "We're going to lose all of the fish if I can't get fuel."

"What about the zoo, how are things there?"

"There's a small group of people keeping the zoo and Audubon Park under control, but I need to find some cops to help out over there, too."

"That's going to be hard, Ron," I confessed. "How did the animals do?"

"Luckily, we didn't lose one big mammal," he replied. "It's strange, but not one tree landed on a single animal's night house."

"No loose lions. That's one piece of good news for the city."

"I've been trying to go back and forth from the zoo to the aquarium, but I ran into problems on Tchoupitoulas Street," he said.

"What happened?"

"A guy pulled a gun on me to try and get my truck," he said. "People will do anything to find a way out of here."

"Ron, security forces with night vision goggles and other equipment are coming to town to deal with this," I said. "You can't be outside at night, OK?" He shook his head.

"Let's write to the kids in Lafayette," I said.

"I thought e-mail wasn't working," Ron said.

"It's not, but we can save it as a draft in case communications start working again," I replied.

"Hi, it's mom AND dad," I wrote. "Daddy got here and is safe and with me now. Phones are getting worse so don't worry if you don't get a call for a couple of days. We are here and with you in our hearts. We love you!!"

We moved back into the Entergy command post and I grabbed my notebook. Bodyguard Louis came inside quickly. "We're moving now!" he commanded as we bolted up and followed him out.

"Louis, please tell me what's happened," I implored, sprinting behind him down the hallway.

"There's a security breach," he said. 'People have scaled the wall in the garage."

"Is there real danger?" I asked.

"Sally, we do not take chances," he replied.

I grabbed Ron to come with us. Inside the stairwell, I drafted a quick pin-to-pin message to Brenda on my Blackberry hoping it would go through. "Urgent!" I wrote. "The buses still aren't here. Security is a big problem. We are moving to the 27th floor for protective purposes."

We began the climb. With us were City Councilwoman Jackie Clarkson, an active mother of five who would fight to the death for her city, Greg the techie, shy TD, bodyguards Wondell and Louis, and two officers outfitted in SWAT gear to protect the Mayor. As we ran up the stairs, I could hardly believe that after enduring five days of hell we were being forced to run for safety inside the hotel. Fear ignited a spring in my step as I jumped two or three stairs at a time.

Running next to Greg and Louis, I wondered if we might need the assistance of a chopper.

"Should we explore the roof?" I asked Louis.

Misinterpreting my request as a mere sightseeing expedition, Greg the techie blurted out, "How about we just worry about Operation Ass-Save right now, Sally?" Perhaps it was the adrenaline, but I broke out laughing at what clearly was not a laughing matter.

When we reached the 27th floor, we entered the Mayor's suite and stared out of the windows onto a city in utter despair. My Blackberry buzzed as I stood next to the window. It was a message from Brenda in Baton Rouge.

> The situation is bad here – riots, robbery, hijacking, closing Baton Rouge City Hall. Mayor needs to call Kip asap. Buses don't want to leave for NO because of safety issues. Gas stations about to close here at noon. Port-o-lets will arrive in the morning and will need escort to Superdome.
>
> Brenda

"More bad news," I told the Mayor. "Brenda said Baton Rouge is descending into chaos and she wants you to call Mayor Holden."

"I've got enough problems here," he replied.

"She says that the buses don't want to come here because of safety concerns, but that port-o-lets will be here tomorrow."

"Yeah, right," the Mayor answered, looking down on the city. The cavalry was not on the streets and the Mayor was getting restless.

"Sally, I want a meeting today with the principals of our command team," he said, referring to Chief Compass, Chief Parent, the Colonel,

Dr. Juliette Saussy, Marcia St. Martin and Chief Matthews. "We need a complete, overall assessment of where we stand."

"You got it," I said.

"I want the team in Baton Rouge getting some things done for us," he said. "We need resources." We compiled a list and sent directions back to Brenda and the team:

> It's 5 days and we still don't have what we need. We are holed up right now and the Mayor wants the team to do the following:
> 1. Focus on supplies running in and out of the city: Diesel fuel, water, food and transport.
> 2. Identify ammunition for police.
> 3. Find us standby airplanes that we can charter at a moment's notice.
> 4. Identify the best in the world at: City planning, architects, levee protection, schools ... just identify, don't contact.
> 5. Put lobbyists to work, then fly to Washington and meet with secretaries of HUD, corps, human services, commerce, energy, interior ... get them thinking about sources of money that they can start to put together for us.
> 6. Get message to President ... We need 250 million federal guaranteed line of credit that we can access immediately to sustain our city.
> 7. Sherry, what is Mayor's authority in relation to FEMA, Governor, and all agencies here and how can he get higher authority. Does his declaration of martial law trump the Governor or others on security and other issues? What tasks can we give other public officials to give them something to do and partially get them out of our way?
> 8. Can we access the cash in the bank for dedicated purposes?

9. Sherry, we have too many people bailing out because of a concern from contractors about liability and can we absolve them for their liabilities other than for gross neglect.
    Thanks guys and we love you all!!!

This was a big list and I realized it would be tough for them to tackle it all. As I stood in the far corner near the window overlooking the city, another e-mail arrived. Tami had found a number for the control booth where WWL radio was operating.

I dialed the number after Greg secured a dial tone. "Garland, how are you, it's Sally." Garland Robinette was the afternoon radio host for WWL and a credible voice in the region.

"I'm fine," he said, happy to hear from us.

"Can you talk? I've got the Mayor."

"Absolutely," he said. The Mayor took the phone and Garland asked him about his conversation with the President from the previous night.

"I told him we had an incredible crisis here and that his flying over in Air Force One does not do it justice," the Mayor answered.

Since that was not what he had said to the President, I gave him a reproachful look. The Mayor turned his back on me and continued talking.

"And they don't have a clue what's going on down here," the Mayor continued. "They flew down here one time two days after the doggone event was over with TV cameras, AP reporters, all kind of goddamn – excuse my French everybody in America, but I am pissed."

I knew the Mayor was referring to the Governor, but I could see how everyone else would think he was talking about the President.

"Now, I will tell you this and I give the president some credit on this," the Mayor said. "He sent one John Wayne dude down here that can get some stuff done, and his name is General Honoré. And he came off the doggone chopper, and he started cussing and people started moving."

"What do you need right now to get control of this situation?" Garland asked.

"I need reinforcements, I need troops, man. I need 500 buses, man," the Mayor said. "We ain't talking about – you know, one of the briefings we had, they were talking about getting public school bus drivers to come down here and bus people out here. I'm like, 'you got to be kidding me, this is a national disaster.' Get every doggone Greyhound bus line in the country and get their asses moving to New Orleans."

"Do you believe that the president is seeing this, holding a news conference on it but can't do anything until Governor Kathleen Blanco requested him to do it?" Garland asked.

"I have no idea what they're doing," the Mayor said. "But I will tell you this: God is looking down on all this, and if they are not doing everything in their power to save people, they are going to pay the price because every day we delay, people are dying and they're dying by the hundreds, I'm willing to bet you."

The Mayor changed the subject. "You know what really upsets me, Garland?" I listened with dread, fully expecting the Mayor to blame the Governor for more deaths. "We told everybody the importance of the 17th Street Canal issue. We said, 'please, please take care of this. We don't care what you do, figure it out.'"

"Who'd you say that to?" asked Garland.

"Everybody: the Governor, Homeland Security, FEMA. You name it, we said it. And they allowed that pumping station next to Pumping Station 6 to go under water," he railed. "And what happened when that pumping station went down, the water started flowing again in the city, and it started getting to levels that probably killed more people.

In addition to that, we had water flowing through the pipes in the city. That's a power station over there. So there's no water flowing anywhere on the east bank of Orleans Parish. So our critical water supply was destroyed because of lack of action."

Oh my goodness, I thought, this is going to cause a war.

"Why couldn't they drop the 3,000-pound sandbags?" Garland asked.

"They said it was some pulleys that they had to manufacture," he said, "but I flew over that thing yesterday, and it's in the same shape that it was after the storm hit. There is nothing happening. And they're feeding the public a line of bull and they're spinning, and people are dying down here."

I motioned again to the Mayor, but he turned his back.

"What can we do here?" Garland sighed.

"Flood their doggone offices with requests to do something, this is ridiculous," the Mayor said. "I don't want to see anybody do anymore goddamn press conferences. Don't do another press conference until the resources are in this city. Don't tell me 40,000 people are coming here. They're not here. It's too doggone late. Now get off your asses and do something, and let's fix the biggest goddamn crisis in the history of this country."

"I'll say it right now, you're the only politician that's called for arms like this," Garland maintained.

"I'm at the point now where it don't matter," the Mayor said. "People are dying. They don't have homes. They don't have jobs. The city will never be the same."

Garland remained silent. "We're both pretty speechless here."

"Yeah, I got to go," finished the Mayor. Welling up, he put the phone down and scurried out of his bodyguard's room.

I sat on the bed and covered my face with my dirty hands.

Several minutes later, I walked into the Mayor's den. He was sitting alone in a club chair.

"Give me some time," he said.

I walked to the elevator bank where Ron stood, staring out on the thousands of people crammed on the Superdome ramp. "What a mess," I said, slipping my hand around his waist, craving a tender touch.

When we were finally given the OK to go downstairs, I went in to the Burgundy Room to get a report from the police. The deputy of public affairs, Paul Accardo, was there, his eyes again glazed in worry.

"What's up, buddy?" I asked.

"I think water is everywhere in the house and got my books and pictures," he said.

"Paul," I answered, "it will be fine." For such a busy cop who was seeing a lot of bad things, he was sounding like a worrywart.

I changed the subject. "Is it true another officer's been shot?"

He mumbled confirmation and began talking about his house again. "Let me know if I can help you, but I've got to go to City Hall right now," I said.

As I walked down the stairwell, my thoughts were on Paul being in such a funk about his house. Not paying attention to my steps, I slipped on something wet. I looked down and screamed, I had just slid on somebody's diarrhea. Jumping out of it, I tried hard not to vomit. Gagging, I ran out of the stairwell and jumped in the water outside of the hotel, ecstatic to be in the dank water rather than the slime inside.

After wading across the sun-drenched street to City Hall, I sat at a desk near the emergency center feeling sick. Put on your alligator skin, I told myself, trying to will away the nausea. Rifling through my notes, I noticed a lone guardsman at a nearby table. We exchanged hellos.

"Where are you assigned?" I asked, happy to turn to mundane afternoon chatter.

"I've been patrolling the streets," he replied. Many National Guard units were beginning to move about the city.

"How are things out there?" I asked.

"I was shot at last night."

"I'm so sorry," I replied in disbelief. "What happened?"

"I was crossing a street and the bullet came pretty close. I've served two times in Iraq and never had a bullet come my way. Now I'm in my own country and I almost get hit."

"Thank God you didn't," I answered.

"I'm not going to die on the streets of New Orleans," he assured me.

I walked back to the Hyatt for our team meeting. Tensions were high as police Chief Compass, Colonel Ebbert, emergency preparedness Chief Matthews, fire Chief Parent, Dr. Juliette Saussy from emergency services, the Mayor and I sat around the table. Mayor Nagin rested his hands on the table and opened the meeting. "I want to see what your most pressing problems are and talk about our priorities," he said.

The Colonel provided an update from the emergency center, where now-satisfied employees had been told their operation would no longer be moving to the Hyatt. "We should have lots of troops arriving in the next several days," the Colonel reported, focusing on the strengths of the battlefield. "Reports have come in of snipers shooting at helicopters trying to land at Charity Hospital," he added, "but we haven't confirmed that."

Chief Compass provided a law enforcement status. "We're arresting people for looting and we're using Union Passenger Terminal as a jail," he said, his gregarious nature now exhausted.

Dr. Saussy and the emergency services team had been conducting non-stop rescues since Monday. "We've got a lot of people still out there," she said, her normally pretty face now haggard.

Chief Parent reported on the fires. "We're trying to fight burning buildings without a water supply," he said. "But we've got helicopters coming in for relief."

At one point in the meeting, as Dr. Saussy spoke, the quick-tempered Colonel discounted her remarks. She closed her mouth and became tight-lipped. After the meeting, I pulled her aside. "Are you OK?" I asked.

"I'm fine," she replied, "I know what we're doing and I'm not going to let that asshole colonel have any effect on me." There was normally a mutual respect between the Colonel and Dr. Saussy, but seasoned pros were nearing breaking points.

"You've seen too much," I said.

"Sally, this is what we do," she replied. "Do me a favor."

"What do you need?" I was eager to help.

"Try not to make me come back here for another meeting again," she said. "I need to be out there with my team rescuing people." She was true grit and I agreed with what she said. I should be out there helping too, I thought.

The Mayor, bodyguards Louis and Wondell, TD and I walked to the heliport for another flyover. TD stood away from the crowd. Walking past the Dome, a number of despondent people pleaded with us again.

"I'm not going to make it and my baby's not going to survive," a grieving mother said as she pushed her baby toward me. The woman seemed close to my own age, with light hair and caramel skin now scorched by the sun. "Please take her." I looked into her pleading eyes.

Her grief ignited a memory of my mother, who had been asked to adopt a handicapped girl. With so many children of her own, my mother declined but lived with the pain of not accepting the child. I now understood how she felt.

"Help will be here soon," I promised as I fought back a well of tears, knowing I could not start accepting babies.

Swarms of people blanketed the Mayor. "Just let me lay down and die," a wrinkled old man said. The Mayor listened closely, hugging them and promising that help would be coming soon. I stormed away, wondering why in the hell these people couldn't be rescued.

The day's flyover showed limited progress. Throughout the sky, helicopters hovered, lifting people to safety. But today was Thursday, almost five days after we had bunkered down, and many people were still in harm's way. I prayed as we flew over for the people still on rooftops and bridges that they would be rescued and wouldn't have to endure another pitch black night outside. "It's so hard to leave the flooded areas at night and hear all the cries for help," one emergency worker told me.

I looked down at a man on a rooftop. A woman and child lay near him while he waved a makeshift flag. I wondered how long he had been waving the flag.

Later, General Honoré came to see us again inside the Entergy command post.

"Mr. Mayor, the nation got your message," he said. I assumed he was referencing the Mayor's interview with Garland Robinette on WWL radio but had no idea how he had heard the local interview.

Months later, Garland explained what happened. "After I interviewed the Mayor," he said, "a CNN van pulled up to our temporary broadcasting booth in Baton Rouge and asked for a copy of the interview. Next thing I know, it's broadcast all over the world."

"Mayor, we're going to overcome this devastating storm that came and flooded the city," General Honoré said. He then mapped out his plan to evacuate the city. "The Superdome evacuation has begun and we should be finished evacuating everything by Saturday, but as fast as we can, we'll move them out."

Better late than never, I thought.

"Phase 1 will start slowly," he said, "but it will build quickly. We are using aircraft and hovercraft-type vessels to evacuate the sick."

I wrote down his plans.

"Buses will transport people from the Dome and the Convention Center," he explained, "and planes will evacuate others. The planes will be flying out of Louis Armstrong Airport. People will not know their destinations, but they will be taken care of when they get to where they're going."

"People won't know where they're going?" I asked.

"Right," the Mayor answered. "They'll have no idea, but they'll be out of here."

Honoré looked at me. "Communications, right?"

"Yes," I answered.

"We need to make the people in the Dome feel good as we get them out of the hell hole," he said. He, too, had witnessed the throngs of people standing cramped together on the Dome's outer ramps. "We need bands." He paused. "And movies playing on big screens to give these people something to do."

I eyed him carefully and wondered how he expected me to secure bands and screens when our city was paralyzed. Hell, I didn't even know the state in which our special events director was living.

"I'll see what I can do," I said, jotting down his request.

Later, I walked over to the Burgundy Room, where Greg's team worked feverishly to get the city wired. Only Big Jim, one of Greg's employees, was there.

"I hear you have some radios," I said, "and I really need one." Big Jim escorted me to a hallway behind the Burgundy Room. He unlocked a large room off of the hallway and shined his flashlight. I was shocked. The room – lined with computers, video games, radios and electronics – looked like a Best Buy.

"Holy Moly, look at all of this," I said, scanning the commandeered loot.

Big Jim handed me a box labeled "weather radio."

"Are you sure a weather radio is going to give me AM radio?" I asked him repeatedly.

"Yes," he assured me. Unfortunately, I would find out later he was wrong.

Chief Riley came back to the Hyatt and entered the Entergy command post with a grim look on his face. "They are not letting people cross the bridge," he said.

"What do you mean?" the Mayor asked. We assumed he was talking about our press release telling people to walk, but the Mayor searched for clarification.

"People started to cross the Mississippi River bridge," Chief Riley said. "Our parish line ends right on the other side of the bridge. The Gretna police stood there with attack dogs and machine guns as people tried to walk."

"Why did they do that?" asked the Mayor.

"Oakwood Mall is burning, and I guess they didn't want anyone else coming into their parish who might do damage."

"But these are people who need to be rescued," the Mayor said. "They were just going to use the bridge as a passageway out of here!"

"Couldn't they just escort them down the highway?" I asked.

"Here we've got people from Plaquemines Parish and St. Bernard Parish being dropped on our highways," the Mayor stormed. Survivors from neighboring parishes had been arriving in New Orleans since rescues began. "We're giving them what little food or water we have and then these people are going to turn away our residents and residents from other parishes with attack dogs? That ain't right!"

I wondered why the police would choose property over people. Then I remembered the Mayor's words: "If they're not here to see this, they have no idea."

The Mayor and I drafted another press release and e-mailed it to Tami. "We are now receiving survivors from Plaquemines Parish who have been transported to New Orleans," we wrote. "We are overwhelmed and out of resources, but we welcome them with open arms and will figure this out together."

Jurisdiction issues with our neighbors to the west weren't the only challenges we faced. Our neighbor to the east, St. Bernard Parish, had reportedly placed cars on bridges to prevent people from getting through, according to Water Board Director Marcia. The St. Bernard Sheriff, Jack Stephens, gave this account to CNN:

> At night, when that sun would go down and the lights were off in the city and all you could see was fires burning along that riverfront and us not being in communication ... we thought the city was burning down. We went to martial law. I gave my deputies full fire authority – anybody that crosses the parish line that does not turn back, we were going to shoot, because this was not going to happen down here.

Before leaving us in the Entergy command post, Chief Riley gave me another list of supplies desperately needed by the police. This list was long: weapons and ammunition, flashlights, rain gear, food and water, the drug Cipro, Augmentin for dysentery, Nexium, Prilosec, Tums, Rolaids, penicillin, Imodium, Cruex, Desenex, underwear, socks, shoes, jeans and undershirts.

I walked in the Burgundy Room to talk to Paul. "Can you look at this and make sure I have everything you need on here?" I asked him.

He stared at me blankly.

"Never mind," I said. "Let me go ask Greg if he can commandeer a drug store for us." Greg was successfully executing all of his heists, except for finding my bullhorns.

Later that night, I saw Doc Stephens. He and the medical staff were still assisting patients inside the Arena adjacent to the Dome.

He hurried toward me with a look of concern. "A real problem is brewing at the Dome," he said.

"Is it a new problem or an old one?" I asked.

"An elderly woman pulled me aside and told me that there was something we had to know," he began. "A group of hoodlums are marking their shirts with a tear in the collar. At noon tomorrow they plan to overtake the guards. They just can't stand it anymore. There's going to be some type of revolt."

"Are you sure of this?" I asked.

"I trust this person who told me," he answered.

I yanked him in to relay the information to the Mayor and Chief Compass, who listened closely.

"We need to get you out of the Dome," said the Mayor. "Get all of the medical staff out of there as soon as possible."

"We still have medical patients there," Doc replied.

"We need to secure the medical teams," the Mayor replied. "They are no good if they become hostages." As Doc crossed back over to the Dome and Arena to round up the medical teams, I felt horrible for the sick people. Maybe our emergency plans had not considered enough the need for massive multiple-day security inside the refuge of last resort. Or maybe this situation was so overwhelming that no one could ever have planned for this.

Later that evening, doctors, nurses and medical assistants moved into the Hyatt. After nearly a week of heroic service to the infirm, they slept on a hard floor.

Before I headed upstairs to bed, I checked in with Doc, who was already at work planning the team's evacuation.

"How's it going?" I asked.

"We're fine, but Sally, are you OK?" Always thinking of others, Doc exuded the warm bedside manner every patient hopes for in a doctor.

"I'm fine." I didn't want to tell him that I had been throwing up every day.

Chapter 8

Showdown on Air Force One

Friday, September 2

As Ron and I slept peacefully on the hotel mattress, I dreamed I was on a beach with waves pounding the sand. The waves soon became rough, so ferocious that I washed out to sea. I felt myself drowning as I woke up to the sound of my Blackberry ringing for the first time in several days. It read 5:30 a.m. as I placed it to my ear.

"Sally?" said a woman's voice.

"Yes," I answered in a daze.

"This is Maggie Grant from the White House." I popped up to turn on a light, forgetting that there was no electricity.

"You're the first call that's come through on my Blackberry," I said. "Who is this again?"

She continued matter-of-factly. "Maggie Grant from the White House."

Shit, I thought, sitting on the edge of the bed while fumbling for a pen.

145

"Sally, we've been meeting about Katrina and understand that the Mayor has not been saying very favorable things about the President for the last 24 hours."

"It's not personal," I answered. "It's been terrible here and we've needed relief for several days now."

"That's exactly why I'm calling you," she said. "The President realizes he may not have gotten accurate information this week and wants to hear directly from the Mayor himself. The President is coming to New Orleans today – could the Mayor meet with him today?"

"Of course," I answered, fumbling for my notebook on the nightstand. I had been speaking for several minutes before Ron finally woke up. "It's the White House," I whispered in his ear.

"May I ask what you do at the White House?" I asked.

"I am the Director of Intergovernmental Relations," she replied.

"OK," I said. "Where do we go from here?"

"Air Force One will be landing this afternoon," she continued. "Jason Recher with White House advance will be calling you with more information as the day proceeds, but here are a few of the specifics." She laid out the protocol of presidential advance as I wrote it all down, understanding more clearly how our President stays protected in this crazy world.

"The President is set to land this afternoon," she continued. "The Mayor's arrival time is actually one hour before the President's arrival time."

"Where will the Mayor be?" I asked.

"We will have him wait on Air Force One for the President to arrive."

"Oh, forgive me for asking," I said, "but is there any way the Mayor could take a shower while he waits? He hasn't showered in days." I figured this could help clear the Mayor's mind after so little sleep.

"Absolutely," she said, surprised but happy to accommodate the request. We talked long enough that I could see Maggie Grant was accomplished and smart. Since I had never read her name in the paper, I concluded she was one of the President's hidden assets.

I got up and walked down to the fourth floor to begin my morning survey. AP reporter Brett Martel, a seasoned reporter not prone to hyperbole, asked "What is the plume of smoke?"

"I didn't see a plume of smoke," I replied. "Are you talking about a plume as in a chemical explosion?"

"Yes I am, and I've heard it's a chemical plant that exploded," he replied. "You didn't feel it rock the building?"

"No, I didn't feel a thing," I said. This was getting crazy, like a scene from "War of the Worlds." I ran to find the Chiefs.

Suddenly, my Blackberry buzzed signaling another message had made it through. It was an e-mail from Economic Development Director Don Hutchinson.

"Harry Connick is on the 'Today' show," he wrote. "He indicated that he could not believe that Mayor Nagin is in Baton Rouge and not in New Orleans. He said if he were mayor he would definitely be in New Orleans."

Where in the heck are people getting their information, I wondered as I hurried to City Hall. Crossing the murky water, it appeared that the water level was going down. I looked to the right and cheered as a long row of buses zigzagged down the street.

At City Hall, I received an update on the chemical explosion. Hazmat was trying to get to the site.

I ran back to the Hyatt, took a deep breath and ran upstairs to the 27th floor to brief the Mayor. "Good morning, Mayor," I said. "There are buses on the street outside and the President is coming in town today and wants to meet with you."

"That's good news," he said.

"I'll give you those details in a minute but here's some bad news," I answered.

"Last night, there was an explosion. All I know is that it was a chemical plant and some people are reporting respiratory and breathing problems. The Fire department can't get to the site. I don't know if Hazmat can get there either. This thing may have to burn out."

The Mayor listened calmly, rubbing an aching knee.

"Also last night, Marcia said people with guns almost overtook the Water Board power plant on the West Bank. She could hear the shots outside and saw people trying to get on the grounds at the perimeter," I said, worry for Marcia on my face. "Mayor, she said it was really scary and that they cannot go through another night like last night."

"I'll give her some extra police," the Mayor said. He picked up his Blackberry and walked to the window, where our chances for getting a clear reception were increasing.

"What else?" he asked.

I continued with the cataclysmic state of the city. "I don't have an update on troops, but I'll try to get that for you."

The Mayor looked for soldiers through the hotel window down to the streets below. "We need to draft another press release," he said. I began to write.

SOS Night of Hell

Last night, our last functioning clean water facility that provides potable water for the West Bank and East Bank of New Orleans was nearly overtaken. If our water supply is further reduced, thousands more will die. One hundred police officers were forced to leave the Convention Center, an area that is critical for 30,000 people.

In the Convention Center, individuals are firing at police officers, but officers cannot return fire because of the fear of hitting civilians in the darkness. Further escalating this crisis, a chemical explosion occurred last night, rocking the downtown area. We are unsure how many people are at risk from the explosion because police and fire cannot access the site with the proper equipment and gear.

I continue to hear that troops are on the way, but we are still protecting this city with only 1,500 police officers, 250 National Guard troops and limited other military personnel primarily focused on evacuation. The people of our city are holding on by a thread.

Over 10,000 people were evacuated yesterday, but we estimate there are 50,000 survivors on rooftops and shelters still needing to be rescued. Time has run out, can we survive another night? Who can we really depend on – only God knows.

"I need to talk to Chief Compass," the Mayor said.

"I'll try to find him for you," I replied, feeling a bit like Paul Revere.

"Now I've got to tell you about the call I got from the White House this morning," I said.

"What happened?"

"The call came in early from the head of Intergovernmental Affairs," I said. "She was very nice and emphasized they wanted to hear from you."

"When does the President come?" he asked.

"We need to leave at noon to arrive at the airport at 12:45. The President will land an hour later," I said. "You will wait for him on Air Force One, where a Colonel Tillman is in charge."

"This is encouraging," he answered.

Eye of the Storm

"I agree. The plan is for you to do a flyover with the President on Marine One," I said. "You might land somewhere downtown and you will definitely stop at the 17ᵗʰ Street Canal."

"Who will be there?" he asked.

"I don't know, but they've asked you to lead the delegation on the ground," I answered. "By the way, they started the conversation saying they know you've been disparaging the President." We chuckled at the uncomfortable situation we were in yet felt encouraged that the President was coming.

"One more thing," I added. "I asked them if there was any way you could shower on the plane since you hadn't had one in a long time and they said yes."

"How's that going to look, Sally? 'He used Air Force One for a shower' is something people could misinterpret," the Mayor said.

"I just thought I'd ask because you had an hour to wait and I thought it would do you good to clear your mind before your meeting."

"I don't know about this one."

"You don't have to do it."

Ron had joined me in the Mayor's suite. "There are a lot of good people trying to help the city," he said to the Mayor. "We can raise a lot of needed money right now."

"What can we do?" the Mayor asked.

"I can get some professional fundraising consultants to donate their time and help organize foundations, governments, local and national leaders and volunteers into a comprehensive plan," he said.

"Write it down," the Mayor said.

When they finished, I turned to the Mayor. "We need to prepare for your meeting with the President," I said, writing a list of possible agenda items: evacuations, 17ᵗʰ Street Canal, pumping help, debris/

150

bodies, landfills, security, letter of credit, support system for displaced residents, schools/medical care/jobs and massive rebuild.

"There's one other thing," I said. "The Speaker of the House, Dennis Hastert, reportedly said maybe New Orleans should not be rebuilt."

"Screw that, we need to counter this," he said. "Think about other natural disasters that affect cities."

"There are plenty," I said.

"Write this down: earthquakes in California, flooding along the East Coast, snowstorms in the Northeast."

"Tornados in the Midwest and heat waves in Chicago," I added, quite sure none of these cities would have to tolerate the Speaker of the U.S. House questioning whether they should be rebuilt.

We headed to the Dome. On the ramp we saw Doug Thornton, the Dome's spiffy executive director, who now seemed shabby and worn.

"Where have you been?" I asked him.

"I've been sleeping here all week," he said. With the help of the Louisiana National Guard and members of the Police Department, Doug had brilliantly kept the battered Dome facilities from completely falling apart. Updating us on the building's structural problems, he led us on a tour of the equipment rooms. "My engineers have been working really hard to keep this generator going," he explained as we walked through the half lit hallways. "The water has seeped through the pilings and the basement is flooding."

"Doug, is there anything we can do to help?" I asked.

"Can you secure some pumps for us?"

"We can certainly try," I answered, as he provided the specifications for the equipment.

We walked inside the offices at the Dome to get an update from police Lieutenant Lonnie Swain. We had reports of numerous crimes being committed and needed to separate fact from fiction.

"There is one serious report of a rape and we are investigating it," Lieutenant Swain said. "We have the guy in custody."

"Good," the Mayor said.

"But Mayor," he added, "we need to get these people out of the Dome." If he only knew how hard we had been trying to do just that. But with phone lines down, police radios jammed and no working satellite phone, there was little more we could do.

Moving to the heliport, we loaded a chopper that would take us to Louis Armstrong International Airport, depositing us on land outside the city limits for the first time since Katrina hit. Upon our arrival, the Mayor was met by the Secret Service and walked over to Air Force One. I was moved to a small building that served as a concourse for the private landing strip. Crossing the airstrip, I noticed the Colonel perched on a suitcase on the tarmac.

I entered the building and my eyes watered when I spotted Brenda, our unassuming head of administration. Denise Bottcher, the Governor's press secretary, and Andy Kopplin, the Governor's chief of staff, stood next to her. Military personnel lined chairs along the walls.

"Oh my God," I cried. "This has been hell." I shared with them what had been happening inside the city while my tears flowed. Andy hugged me and Denise comforted me. Brenda, having never seen me cry, observed carefully as if ensuring that my faculties were still intact.

"I'm fine," I assured her. "It's just hard to believe what's happened."

The four of us moved to one of the official White House RVs. The motor home was souped up and the air conditioning felt refreshing on my face. There were beds, televisions, cold bottled water and snacks.

There was also a phone on board, but it only dialed federal agencies in Washington. We sat down on the jump sofas. Andy was agitated that he and Brenda, as the official seconds-in-command for the state and city, had not been allowed to board Air Force One. I asked the Secret Service agent inside the RV to get agent Jason Recher from the White House advance office on the phone for me.

"Jason's not available right now," he replied. I could tell he was stalling.

Outside of the RV, the Colonel had left his suitcase perched on the tarmac and was now asleep on top of the concrete landing strip.

The President arrived on Marine One and was shuffled immediately onto Air Force One. Inside the RV, we watched TV coverage of the events that were unfolding on the runway directly in front of us.

After a while, the congressional delegation left Air Force One and walked over to the choppers waiting to do a flyover of the city. The Mayor, Governor and President were not with the group. A few minutes later, the President and the Mayor emerged.

"There they are," I said, as the President and Mayor walked to Marine One.

Denise noticed the Governor was not with them and quickly pulled Andy aside. "The Governor's not part of the group!" she urgently whispered. She picked up her phone to place a call as she moved to the back of the RV.

"Sally, I need to talk to you now," Andy said. "This is so wrong."

"What is so wrong?" I asked.

"For the last several days I have been reading the Posse Comitatus Act all through the night and I promise you that this is all about politics," he said.

"Posse what?" I asked, laughing at the sound of the word.

"Posse Comitatus," he said.

"What on earth is that?" I asked.

"It means that the military can't perform law enforcement duties," he said. Suddenly, he pointed to the ceiling and whispered, "Wait, come outside, this RV is probably bugged."

"Come on, Brenda," I said as we moved outside.

Huddling on the tarmac, Andy informed us about the Posse Comitatus Act, which generally limits the federal government from using the military for law enforcement.

"The military does not enjoy such rights," he said. "I've read this and it's clear the state should be in charge," he argued. "The feds are trying to screw us," he said.

"It's not important who is doing law enforcement," I replied. "What's important is that help gets inside the city and quick."

Andy agreed, but the handwriting was on the wall. Politics was playing into their decision making.

Denise walked outside to clarify that the Governor had boarded Marine One ahead of the President. "She is with the President," she said. Denise had reacted the same way I would have if the Mayor had been excluded.

For the next hour, we sat in the RV and talked about the status of the city. Andy explained the challenges with the buses.

"FEMA told us they had the buses. We completely trusted them. Finally, we just took matters into our own hands and started getting school buses from around the state."

"We're just so happy to finally have them there," I replied.

After a tour of the city, the presidential choppers arrived back at the airport. We walked over to the tarmac near Air Force One. As officials exited the choppers, I saw U.S. Senator Mary Landrieu. We hugged.

With the President standing just behind her, the Senator told me, "Norma Jane and Madeleine know more about recovery than this

President," referring respectively to her chief of staff in Washington and her sister, a New Orleans judge and my former college roommate. I was sure the President could easily overhear the Senator's stern words.

"Mary, how did everyone fare in the storm?" I asked, changing the subject.

"Madeleine lost her house, Martin lost his house, the camp is gone," she said, talking about her siblings' and parents' homes. Like practically everyone, she had terrible tales of destruction.

The President moved to a podium as the other officials gathered behind him. The delegation seemed in sync after the tour, nodding in affirmation at the President. I stood at the rope and stanchion, listening closely to the President's message.

"The Governor and Mayor of New Orleans, Senator Landrieu, Senator Vitter and Congressman Jefferson, Congressman Jindal and General Blum and I have just completed a tour of some devastated country," the President began. "I want to thank the Governor for her hard work, and I want to thank the Mayor. St. Charles, St. Bernard, Plaquemines Parish, I understand the devastation that you've gone through as well."

"St. Tammany," the Governor added, interrupting the President.

"One of the objectives that we had today," the President continued, "was to move in and secure that Convention Center, and make sure the good folks there got food and water." Oddly, the President was looking right at me. Then I remembered my son McClain's Longhorns cap on my head. He thinks I'm a Texan, I chuckled.

"The Mayor has been telling me, not only by telephone, but here in person, how important it is that we get that breach filled and get that pump station up and running."

Good. The Mayor had clearly conveyed his most important message: to finally close that breach so that the lake would stop flowing into the city.

"I believe that the great city of New Orleans will rise again and be a greater city. I believe the town where I used to come to enjoy myself, occasionally too much, will be that very same town, that it will be a better place to come."

The audience laughed. Chances were pretty strong that if you had been to New Orleans, you had played in New Orleans.

"I understand we've got a lot of work to do," he said. "May God bless the people of this part of the world, and may God continue to bless our country."

Did he really understand how much work we've got to do, I wondered.

As we walked away from Air Force One, I saw Congressman Bobby Jindal, a Rhodes scholar and former assistant secretary of the U.S. Department of Health and Human Services.

"This was crazy, Sally," he said. "When we met on the plane, the President offered the Governor and the Mayor a plan to send in the resources and help but the Governor told both the President and the Mayor that she needs time to think about it."

"What?" I asked incredulously.

"The Mayor will tell you. The Governor said she needs 24 hours," he repeated.

Was the Governor paralyzed with fear? As General Patton had said, "Lead me, follow me, or get out of my way," but I wondered which of these courses she could possibly be charting.

After the President left, the Mayor spoke briefly to Lieutenant General H. Steven Blum, head of the U.S. National Guard. After their visit, we walked back to the RV.

Agent Jason approached with a more accommodating message. "The White House would like to send a Communications team back into the city with you," he said. "Would that be helpful?"

"It certainly would," I replied. "At least we can reach the White House when we need to."

The Mayor, Brenda, the Colonel and I gathered behind the RV. Cameramen and reporters soon converged on the Mayor. I looked over my shoulder. The Governor and her entourage were driving away. But within minutes of passing by us, the Governor's car turned back so she could join the Mayor at the cameras.

Back inside the chopper, the Mayor said, "Man, you wouldn't believe what happened."

"Tell me," I probed.

"When we get back."

We arrived back at the heliport and got into a Humvee to drive back down to the Hyatt. Driving on the ramp through the evacuees, I saw a shirtless young boy peering through the railings of the barricade. Beside him, a family sat under a light blue blanket perched atop two chairs, reminding me of the tents we made as kids.

We rounded the corner of the outer ramp. A pale man with red hair and a long beard was climbing up onto the ledge of the Dome's walkway. Surely if he fell, he would die. As we realized his intent was to jump, two guardsmen ran to stop the man from committing suicide. As we called out, others tried to save him. One of the guards lunged and caught the man by his legs in the nick of time.

Back at the hotel, we sat in the atrium lobby as the Mayor filled me in on what had transpired on Air Force One.

"When I first met the President he told me he heard that I had been saying things about him."

"Was that freaky?" I asked.

"Not really," he answered. "I told him I was sorry and that I had been caught up in the moment. He told me they could have done better. He said what was important was how we moved forward.

"Then we flew out to the 17th Street Canal. We got out and walked around. You should see it."

"How does it look?"

"A little better," he answered. "I really wanted to see what it looked like from the ground level so I walked all around out there. I even jumped on a wall so I could see over to the other side of the lake."

"Was there still a lot of debris?"

"Yeah. But the funny thing was the President kept coming over to walk with me," the Mayor added. "I kept hearing him say, 'where's the Mayor?' as he walked around."

"He probably wanted you next to him in the photos," I said.

"Listen, this is funny," he said. "At one point, I had walked over to the breach and was completely apart from the President. The Secret Service ran up. They said the President wanted to know where I was," the Mayor explained. "The Secret Service asked me to walk with the President to point things out. But I had moved pretty far away and he really wanted me to catch up with the President. The agent asked, 'Mr. Mayor, can you jog?' I said yes and I jogged back over to the President."

"That is so funny." I pictured the Mayor running over to the President and remembered that his knee had been swelling up. "How'd your knee feel?"

"It was fine," he said.

"Later on in Air Force One we had this big meeting with all the congressmen and Landrieu and Vitter and Andy Card," he continued, referring to our U.S. senators and the President's chief of staff.

"I heard they wouldn't let Charlie Melancon in," I said, the Democratic congressman perhaps too much of a thorn in the President's side.

"So we are having this meeting and it's going around the table and everybody's saying what they think the problems are," the Mayor said. "Chain of command came up. I was advocating a clear chain of command to get resources flowing in the right places."

I pictured the inside of Air Force One, full of Louisiana legislators moving back and forth from room to room where Ford, Carter, Reagan and Clinton had worked.

"Everybody was talking but nobody was getting anywhere. Finally I got rather forceful and told the President and the Governor that they needed to figure out who was in charge. They both agreed that they would work on it," the Mayor explained. "I said 'I mean today, now.' I told them we all would leave the room so the two of them could work it out."

"What happened next?"

"I think the President was a little caught off guard at how direct I was," the Mayor said, "but then he said 'No, there's a bunch of you in this room and only two of us, we'll leave the room.' Apparently when the President talked to the Governor alone, he gave her some ways to get it done."

The Mayor took a deep breath. "This is what is so unbelievable," he said. "The President called me in that office after that and said, 'Mr. Mayor, I offered two options to the Governor. I was ready to move today but the Governor said she needed 24 hours to make a decision.'"

"Jindal mentioned this," I said.

"Can you believe it? He actually came back to her with a workable plan and she told him she needed 24 hours to think about it."

"I think this has something to do with this federal act called Posse Comitatus," I said.

"I don't get it for any reason," he said. "She could have owned this. She could have walked out on that tarmac with the President and said 'we have a solution to the problems' and she would have been the hero."

Having no idea why the Governor would have made that call, I tried to lighten the tension. "Did you get to shower on Air Force One?"

"Yep," he said. "There was this brother from Brooklyn who was the steward on the plane. He set me up for the shower – not in the guest bathroom but in the President's bathroom. It felt so good that when he first knocked on the door to tell me that the President was arriving, I said OK but I just let the warm water continue to fall – it felt so good. It was only when the second set of knocking occurred and I heard, 'Sir, the President has arrived and they are waiting for you to begin the meeting,' that I knew I had to get out of there quick."

I laughed. Suddenly, a movement caught my eye. A face peered at us through a potted plant. "May I help you with something?" I asked.

"Yes, you may. I'm Mary Claude Foster, Ted Koppel's producer," the woman said, coming from behind the palm and plopping at the table where we were meeting. "Ted Koppel is the number one news show and the number one nighttime news magazine. We would like the Mayor to appear with John Donvan on the Ted Koppel show and on a town hall meeting later next week with Ted."

"I'll talk to you shortly," I told her. "Right now we are meeting."

"Well, we're the program that is going to let you talk to America and we want to do a town hall meeting with the Mayor."

"Please, give us some time," I asked. "We are dealing with so many challenges and the last thing on our mind right now is town hall meetings."

"I will, but first I need to know if you will ... "

"I'm asking you to give us time," I interrupted.

"I've not seen you get mad like that," the Mayor said as the producer walked away.

Soon, Hyatt General Manager Michael Smith walked over. "How would you like a hot meal?" he asked. My stomach was growling.

"Man, I would love that," the Mayor answered, "but could you give some to the people left around here, too?"

"We've already taken care of that," he said. He was a first-class manager, never failing to take care of his guests despite the unbearable conditions in the hotel.

Scott Pelley from "60 Minutes" appeared after we ate and asked, "Can I have the Mayor?"

"Let me see if he's up to it," I replied. "Maybe you can join us on a flyover tomorrow." The Mayor still wanted to approve each interview.

Later that day, the police chiefs came to the Entergy command post to discuss evacuation of the city since our criminal justice system, water system and public security were, in effect, no longer functioning.

"We're going to have to empty the city completely and enforce the mandatory evacuation," the Mayor said. Discussions followed about whether force should be used to pull people out of their homes.

"I don't want anyone to be removed forcefully," the Mayor said.

I crossed the hallway to the Burgundy Room to share the news about the added technology assistance. "Greg, the White House has sent a Communications team here to work with you," I said. "It's two guys with short hair, they look somewhat alike. I told them to look for you."

"Whatever," he said, as if his competency was being questioned.

That evening, General Honoré came back to the Hyatt and pulled out a chair at the round table in the Entergy command post. "The evacuations have begun and are proceeding smoothly," he said, continuing to size up the Mayor's enigmatic personality.

He presented us a hand-written note that read: "As of 0700 to present: Citizens who departed Superdome today: 9,275. Citizens who remain: 2,700. Buses utilized: 265."

However, flocks of new survivors from all over the region had begun to pour into the Dome.

Later on in the Mayor's suite, I ran through my notes as TD sat quietly in a chair next to the wall. The Mayor stood up and breathed a deep sigh as he looked out of the window at the darkened sky.

"Are you OK?" I asked him.

"This was God's plan for me, Sally," he said.

"What was?" I asked.

"To rebuild New Orleans."

With Ron at the aquarium, I roamed around the hotel, heading to the sixth floor where Greg the techie and a few of his team members huddled with vendors from Unisys, a contractor Greg had engaged to help with communications. They were working on phones and computers as cables weaved through several rooms. As the techies worked, they shared a bottle of whiskey in the darkened hall.

I walked through their work area when a FEMA representative approached me. "We need to meet with the Mayor," he said.

"How about tomorrow?" I asked.

"No, it's urgent," he said.

I ran up the stairs to retrieve the Mayor and brought him back to the sixth floor.

Big Jim, the techie who had told me the weather radio would work as a transistor radio, had a nearby fan blowing. "Big Jim, can we meet in here?" I asked.

"Sure," he answered as he positioned the fan for the Mayor.

Phil Parr and his colleague came in and sat down on one of the beds, their FEMA polo shirts still crisp. I leaned against the credenza in the room and pulled out my notebook. The Mayor took a seat on the bed opposite them. With the heat and late night hour, I felt my clammy body fading off.

"We have a few problems," Parr began. "If you enforce the mandatory evacuation to ensure that everyone evacuates the city, FEMA will no longer be able to provide food for people in New Orleans."

"This is a joke, right?" I asked, waking right back up. But it wasn't. The Mayor listened intently as Parr laid out the latest technical provisions of FEMA by which we were supposed to abide.

I could scarcely believe they were not going to provide food on a technicality. Almost a week after the storm, FEMA was still telling us what they could not do.

After finding a room to crash that night, I struggled to sleep. The cavalry had arrived but bureaucracy was still tightening like a noose around our necks.

Chapter 9

Is this Really America?

Saturday, September 3

I woke up with a better feeling, hopeful that everyone would be rescued today. Ron and I walked down the hall into a room facing the French Quarter. We noticed unbroken water bottles in the minibar and stepped carefully over shards of glass to get them. There was only one salvageable bottle. We opened it up and tiptoed closer to the window to feel the breeze from the missing wall.

"Oh no!" I screamed as we looked to the right. Thick white smoke filled the sky. "It looks like the French Quarter is on fire."

"It looks like the aquarium," Ron howled as he ran out. "I've got to go."

I walked quickly down to the Hyatt plaza breezeway where thousands of people were filing out to waiting buses on the street below. In front of me, a large pear-shaped woman grabbed her two young children, one by the arm and the other by the hand, marching them through the crowded hallway with a tattered black purse strapped across her shoulder. Near the line, armed guardsmen stood watch, handing out water as people moved to the waiting buses.

A young girl nearby held onto a mutt with a shaggy tan coat.

"You can't take your pets," an officer told her.

"Why not?" she cried.

"We're not allowing pets on the buses," he said, taking the squeamish dog from her arms. The little girl cried but no one comforted her. I turned away.

As I walked upstairs, I felt the now familiar pit in my stomach.

The Mayor asked me to gather everyone for a noon meeting. "I'm going to make all of our chiefs and all of the city employees that have been in town cycle out of the city," he said. "They're not going to want to do it, but they're exhausted and need some sleep to be effective."

"OK," I said, jotting it down.

"I need you to help me push this," he said. I realized this was going to be a tough conversation.

Ron came in to the Mayor's suite. "It wasn't the aquarium that was on fire," he said.

"I heard it was Saks," I said.

"As tragic as this is," Ron said to the Mayor, "it's also an incredible opportunity to fix the schools and plan for the future."

"Write down your plan," the Mayor replied. Ron began to plot out everything the city would need to recover: architects and planners, timelines and goals.

When they finished collaborating, Ron got up. "Sally, I'm going back to the aquarium," he said. "There are two policemen working hard to keep the sea otters alive, but I need to go back and help them." The sea otters were the only endangered species at the aquarium. "We're losing a lot of fish," he added.

"That's so sad," I said, kissing him goodbye. "Go."

166

The Mayor walked over to check on the small fish he was watching for his young daughter. "My fish is doing well," he said.

"Good," I said.

Greg the techie entered the room. "Andy Card is trying to reach you," he told the Mayor. We headed to the sixth floor area where we had been with FEMA just a few hours before. Greg handed us a cordless telephone to dial the number I had been given.

"This is Sally Forman with Mayor Nagin in New Orleans," I said, leaning out of a blown-out window to aid reception. "We're trying to reach Mr. Card."

I handed the phone to the Mayor. "Andy, how are you?" the Mayor said. "Yes, I had a good meeting with the President." The Mayor then reiterated his federal request to patch the levee and get evacuation resources. He hung up the phone.

"Things are looking up?" I asked.

"Yes," he answered.

At noon, we gathered in a circle in the fourth floor hallway in the Hyatt. "I want each of you to know," the Mayor said, "that I am now holding General Honoré accountable for the evacuations and security in the city. This will give each of you a chance to get your departments collected and make the assessments of where each department and agency stands."

Everyone nodded in agreement.

"Now I want to talk to each of you about taking some time off," he said. "You're tired and you need some rest."

As expected, none of them wanted to leave.

Chief Parent was the first to concede. "I've had someone standing with me the last couple of days watching me as I make decisions because I know I have not slept enough," he said. "I need someone else checking to make sure my decisions are sound."

"Good," said the Mayor. "Now let's go around and talk about where each department stands."

We ran through the status of all of the departments as I carefully took notes.

> Fire – Assistant Chief Holmes will take over for 3 days. Give all firefighters 7 days off in rotation and check on the Credit Union.
>
> Emergency center – There's a new team coming in to replace the team on duty since the storm began. We need to transfer the phone system to a switchboard in another state for available communications. We need a new location for the burgeoning center.
>
> Water Board – The City of Lafayette is sending in an assessment team. Six pump stations are up and running. We need a trailer city for employees.
>
> Police – Chief Riley is working on who's here, who isn't. Housing is needed for over 80 percent of the force. Officers need to see their families.
>
> Homeland Security – The Colonel said he was there to stay and his team would not leave their posts. *Note to self: convince him later.*
>
> Mayor/Sally – Mayor needs to thank emergency center team. Rebuild the fire department. Repair the Florida Avenue breaches in the levee. Establish a new central command. Create a database of city employees. Help responders on duty since before the storm.

I verified the notes as the Mayor made a startling comment. "We really need all of you to leave," he said. "We can't afford to have any more suicides like Paul and the other cop."

"Paul who?" I asked. Everyone looked at me.

"Sally, you don't know?" the Mayor said. "Paul Accardo."

"Oh my God, no!" I screamed, unable to fathom the news. "Where's Marlon?" I cried. He stood hunched in the hallway, leaning over the balcony and I ran to him in tears.

"Marlon, I'm so sorry," I said, hugging him tightly. "Poor Paul!" Marlon's wide shoulders began shaking in deep despair, his trusted assistant and dear friend killed by the madness of Katrina and its aftermath.

"What happened?" I asked.

"He shot himself," he said. I held him as we cried.

"I'm so sorry," I whispered, "life is so unfair." Old pain from my sister's and father's deaths from cancer returned. As we stood in silent grief, my heart broke for Paul's family, for Marlon and for all of us.

My head pounded as I dried my tears and got back to stabilize essential city departments. I could hardly concentrate as the meeting wound down. I had spent the week with Paul, sharing the challenges of trying to help a city that was cut off at its knees. Paul's zoning out had been a cry for help but I had dismissed his worries and ignored his losses. Now I wondered how I could have been so blind.

Damn this senseless death, I screamed inside. Damn, damn, damn.

When the meeting ended, a heavily built Homeland Security employee from Atlanta approached. The agent had been trying unsuccessfully to meet with the Mayor for days. I felt badly about the seeming lack of courtesy, but I had a strong sense that we would be disappointing a lot more people in the coming months.

Down the hall, I noticed Congressman Bill Jefferson, a Democrat from New Orleans. Later, I said hello as I passed him in the hallway. Congressman Jefferson introduced me to a representative from Jani-King, a janitorial supply company, who that had accompanied him. The vendor was pleasant but began to follow the Mayor and me around. After a while, I turned to the man from Jani-King. "Sir, how can I help you?"

"I'm here to do whatever you or the Mayor needs – anything at all," he said. "I'll even run get your drinks."

"Thanks, but that's not necessary," I said.

Later, the Mayor pulled me aside. "Stay away from him," he said.

"Who?" I asked. The FBI had recently raided Jefferson's home, but he had not yet been charged with anything.

"Jeff," he said in reference to the Congressman. "I don't trust him."

Later, Mayor Nagin would endorse Congressman Jefferson in his reelection bid, just a few months before the federal government handed down an indictment charging Jefferson with multiple counts of bribery, obstruction of justice, wire fraud, money laundering and racketeering.

"Sally, come quick, your husband's in trouble," a man said as I rounded a corner in the hotel. "They were testing the elevator on the new generator and your husband got in it unaware they were testing it out." This did not sound good, I thought. "He's stuck between the 14th and 15th floors."

I ran to the atrium lobby and looked up. Ron was peering out of the glass elevator. I scampered up the stairs now covered with excrement, my dirty T-shirt covering my nose. Reaching him, I sat down next to the closed elevator doors and saw a tiny gap. "Ron, touch my finger," I said. His finger appeared through the small crack.

Hyatt security arrived and tried to pry the doors open. A hotel engineer rushed onto the scene. "You are making a big mistake," he said. "Opening the door could sever him in two."

I hurried down to find General Manager Michael Smith. "Michael, Ron is caught in your elevator," I stuttered.

"I'm sorry," he said. "We were trying to start it up with a small generator and it broke."

"What can we do to get him out?" I asked.

"We have to get a part to fix the elevator, and the closest supplier is in Baton Rouge," he said.

"How long will it take?"

"We will get him out in three or four hours," he assured me. I ran back up to the 15th floor.

"What am I looking at here," he said. "I want the truth."

"Four hours at the most," I told him. He recognized the helplessness of his position and lay down on the floor of the elevator. I thought about our state of affairs: Ron was trapped, Paul was dead and the city was in chaos. Miserable doing nothing, I walked back downstairs.

With Ron lying on the elevator floor perched 15 floors above us, we conducted a "60 Minutes" interview in the atrium lobby with Scott Pelley. I looked up constantly as the disheveled Mayor talked about draining the city and collecting the dead.

After the interview, I saw Greg. "How are the two people from White House communications working out?"

"Man, those dudes are spies," he said placing his hands on his hips.

"What?" I asked, surprised.

"They are putting bugs all over this place," he said, "and they don't know shit about technology." I doubted this was true but Greg certainly believed it. Now we have spies to contend with, I thought.

Earlier in the morning, we had been told that actors Sean Penn and Steven Seagal were in town. Someone handed me a note that Harry Connick Jr. was on the street waiting to see the Mayor.

"Not interested," the Mayor said, remembering Connick's bogus remarks about him not being in the city.

Later that day, the Mayor received a hand-written apology from the New Orleans born singer. "I'm sorry I said on national television that you were in Baton Rouge," he began. "I appreciate the fact that you were in New Orleans helping our city."

"At least he had the class to say he was sorry," I said. Later, Connick would express his regard for his hometown by helping to create homes for musicians through Habitat for Humanity.

After two hours inside the glass enclosure, the Hyatt engineer safely removed Ron from the elevator. He was freed.

I spotted Soraya, Chief Matthew's assistant in the emergency center. "I think the worst is over," I said.

"Hopefully that's true," she replied. "By the way, I've been looking for you," she added. "Sarah Fulton called. Secretary Chertoff would like to meet with the Mayor at 8:30 a.m. tomorrow at Zephyr Field."

"Tell them we'll be there," I said, thanking her.

Walking across the Dome ramp that morning, I noticed a large American flag the National Guard had draped near the ramp. Scanning the debris field of dirty blankets, luggage and excrement, I turned to face the flag and asked aloud, "Is this really America?"

As I walked on, a National Guardsman recognized me. "Can I talk to you?" he asked.

"Of course."

"The Guard units are very upset because they heard the Mayor in an interview saying that the Guard was not here."

"The Mayor meant full-scale enforcements were not here at that time," I explained. "I'm sorry that it came across that way to you. We really appreciate the service you're providing to the city." As I left, I made a note to have the Mayor thank the Guard units.

On the horizon, a new cloud of black smoke blew. I ran to the Hyatt to find out what was burning.

"Louis, can you drive me on the dry streets in Big Daddy?" I asked, since Ron now had my truck.

"Sure," he replied. We headed Uptown toward the fire burning on a flooded street in the Lower Garden District. A large wall of flames engulfed several buildings, demonstrating how easily the whole city could burn down. Inching closer, we spotted two firefighters battling the inferno using floodwater from the street.

"What a sight," I said.

"That's the biggest fire I've ever seen," Louis concurred.

Back at the hotel, bottles of water sat inconspicuously in a hallway. I grabbed three, hoping to use them to take a shower. Inside my room, I jumped into the tub.

"Crud," I cried. Three bottles were not nearly enough to shower.

"I have never craved a cold shower so badly in my life," I later told the Mayor and bodyguard Louis.

"You need to use the back of the toilet," the Mayor explained. "That's three liters of clean water."

"Gross," I replied, but my current hygiene was indeed fouler than clean toilet water.

I received word that Amtrak was telling the press they had called the city on the Saturday before Katrina hit to offer a train to help evacuate citizens, but that their offer had been declined.

"Check the story out," the Mayor directed me.

"Chief, what happened?" I asked Chief Matthews later. "There's a report that Amtrak spoke to you about evacuations and you declined the help."

"I don't remember that," he said, eyeing me above his bifocals.

I relayed the message. "Chief Matthews said he does not recollect the conversation with Amtrak."

"Call Amtrak and check it out," the Mayor said. "No rush."

"May I speak to Cliff Black?" I asked weeks later, having secured a number for Amtrak's Vice President of Public Relations. After I explained who I was and why I was calling, he informed me that his colleague, Josie Harper, had worked with Chief Matthews in the past. "She personally called on Saturday afternoon before the storm to tell the Chief that there were available seats on a train for those needing to evacuate," Mr. Black said. At that point, it was clear a lack of planning on our part had hindered this type of critical help.

As we flew over the city that morning, the success of the air evacuations was apparent. Reports of over 150,000 survivors evacuated by air and boat were being tossed around the heliport with pride.

Later, the Mayor turned to me. "Sally, maybe you should leave."

"What do you mean?" I asked.

"This job might be too big for you," he said.

"What are you implying?" I asked. His words shocked me, as if I were being cut from the team. "Are you unhappy with something?"

"No, I'm not unhappy," he said. "I just think this is going to take a lot out of you and maybe you should just go be with your family."

I protested. "I appreciate your concern but I'm fine unless you would rather someone else come in and do this job." We let it drop.

Late that evening, the Mayor, Louis, Wondell, TD and I drove to the nearly empty Convention Center. Geraldo Rivera was standing on top of a trailer across the street with a klieg light shining on him. Food and water crates were now piled on street corners. If the resources had arrived sooner, there would have been no Geraldo. At 10:30 p.m., the last bus took off with scared faces peering through the windows.

Back at the hotel, we searched for rooms in which to sleep. General Manager Michael Smith located a few clean rooms for us in the nearby tower. Reaching into his pocket, TD wiped his hands with a clean white handkerchief.

"I want to meet about something," the Mayor said. It was 1 a.m. and I was exhausted.

"Now?" I asked.

"We can do it," TD answered.

We walked into the Mayor's suite. "Sally, I want to cycle out *all* of our first responders," he began. "They also have worked too hard and too long and need a mental break."

"OK, what do you want to do?"

"Let's connect them to their families first and then send them somewhere where they can temporarily forget about all this."

"What are you thinking?" I asked.

"Call Herb Kelleher from Southwest Airlines and the Mayor of Las Vegas, Oscar Goodman, and Shirley Franklin in Atlanta and work out a plane and a trip."

"OK," I said. I was so exhausted my muscles ached.

"And before the first responders go anywhere, I want them to have a complete physical and a psychological evaluation in Baton Rouge," he added. "We don't need any more suicides."

"Mayor," I said. "I need to tell you something. This is a huge job, it's almost two in the morning and I do not have enough energy to be a travel agent and event planner right now." Pain continued to develop in my bones. "Can I give all of this to Sherry?"

"Sure," he said. "But you make the call to Southwest and get the mayors on the phone for me."

Later, Herb Kelleher from Southwest Airlines, along with several other airlines, jumped at the opportunity to help our first responders. Mayor Goodman, Mayor Franklin, Houston Mayor Bill White and several other mayors also offered support. "I owe you some gumbo," the Mayor told each of them gratefully for bolstering our sagging team.

Back in the Mayor's suite, I secured a line and called Sherry. The phones were still hit and miss. "I need you big time," I said.

"Fire away," she said, jotting everything down with her usual flair for tough assignments.

"Now we're talking," said the Mayor. He was thrilled to be helping the men and women who had worked so hard in the city. "Once they leave the airport," he said, knowing sick people covered the terminal floors, "they won't have to think about the nightmare again until they return."

Despite our best efforts, the plan for first responders to fly to Vegas or other cities became a procedural mess that the Colonel would later sum up: "Great idea but bad timing."

It was after 2 a.m. before we finally left the Mayor's room. I moved to my room and immediately thought about my family. One hundred forty miles away, my son was writing a note. "Dear Mom and Dad," he wrote. "I can't wait to see you. I can't wait to have a normal life again. This is so crazy. Love, McClain."

Chapter 10

Chertoff's Snub

Sunday, September 4

Matt Zimmerman, a young NBC producer, was building a name for himself as "Mr. Persistence," so I agreed to bring the Mayor to the hotel plaza breezeway for an early morning interview on the "Weekend Today" show.

"Mayor, how did you sleep?" I asked.

"Much better," he said.

The hotel was now clear of evacuees and I relished the relief. As the Mayor miked up, two stray dogs wandered through the plaza breezeway. The producer gave the Mayor a thumbs up as the interview began.

"Mr. Mayor, I was appalled by the conditions that I saw at the Convention Center. Can you explain to us how something like this can happen in the city of New Orleans?" asked anchor Campbell Brown.

"You know, I can't explain it," he said. "If you think that's bad, you should go take a tour of the Superdome."

Then the host hit him hard. "Well, why didn't you do anything? You're the mayor of this city."

"I made calls to everybody—the president, all of his Cabinet members that were associated with providing resources, FEMA officials, the Governor," he said. "The bottom line is the help did not come, and we had 1,500 police officers that held this city together for at least three days."

"That sounded like a cheap shot," I told the producer when the interview ended. Campbell Brown's father, Jim Brown, was the Democratic insurance commissioner in Louisiana before going to jail for lying to the FBI and I wondered if her view of the Mayor was already tainted.

"I'll check it out," the young producer replied.

I looked over and noticed the stray dogs making their way toward bodyguards Louis and Wondell, who were leaning on chairs while the Mayor conducted his interview. With his muscular forearm, Wondell swiped one of the wild mutts away.

"Don't do that," I scolded him. "These dogs are so scared."

"I'm not going to be friends with that dog," he yelled back at me.

We left the plaza breezeway and walked over to the rooms housing the National Guard unit from New Mexico. The Mayor walked through the crowd, shaking hands and assisting in damage control as he thanked the guardsmen.

As we departed, a small group of people, looking like they had just arrived in the city because of their clean appearance, converged upon the Mayor. "We need to talk to you," a man said as he approached the Mayor. Louis and Wondell moved in closer.

"That's fine," the Mayor said.

Inside an adjacent room, the Mayor was introduced to a middle-aged man in a short-sleeve sport shirt and freshly ironed pants, wearing a determined look. As the man spoke, the Mayor listened with a hint of suspicion on his face.

As I stood outside the room, two armed men in black uniforms approached me. The word ICE was written across their jacket. "We're federal agents and we've been assigned to watch the Mayor," they said.

"Great, thanks," I said. "You'll need to talk to Louis and Wondell to work it out."

Louis and Wondell later fussed at me. "We decide who secures the Mayor, not you."

"Sorry," I said. "I was just thanking him for the help."

When we left the room, the Mayor sidled up next to me.

"Did you see that guy who was talking to me?" he whispered.

"Who was he?" I asked.

"His name is James Lee Witt and the Governor hired him to take control of the situation," he said.

"Is he good?"

"He's Clinton's guy and he just gave me all this bull about Bush," he said, forming his battle lines. "I don't trust that guy."

"Why not?" I asked.

"The President has the money and I'm not going to get caught in this trap," he continued. "This is people trying to run a national election from our catastrophe."

The last thing we needed right now was "party crap" infiltrating our recovery. I had already received messages that James Carville, Jesse Jackson and Rudy Giuliani were trying to reach the Mayor and hoped their motives were altruistic.

We headed to the heliport to fly to our early morning meeting with Secretary Chertoff. The Colonel met us there.

We landed on the Saints practice field next to the minor league baseball stadium Zephyr Field. Two bent goalposts rested on the otherwise pristine, manicured greens. The Mayor, Colonel, Louis,

Wondell and I walked the grounds looking for Secretary Chertoff, at this point nowhere in sight. We walked over to the Saints administration building and didn't see him there. Groups of people were gathered a half a mile away, so we hiked down the long road to meet them. As we got closer, we spotted Secretary Chertoff with FEMA Director Michael Brown. Chertoff was wrapping up a remote interview that we would later learn was a grilling from Tim Russert on "Meet the Press."

Although Chertoff saw that we had arrived for the meeting, after a quick handshake, the Secretary walked off with his entourage in tow. Assuming we should follow, I walked beside the Mayor and the Colonel in the direction of the delegation. A press pool followed the group in front, taking pictures of the Mayor walking behind them and the Secretary ahead of them. Oddly, Secretary Chertoff did not approach.

As we rounded a bend and came upon a parking lot, our eyes nearly popped out of our heads. Covering the massive parking lots were boats and pumps and lights, loads of reinforcements and equipment, all sitting on the ground waiting to be used. This was exactly what we had been begging for all week. How long had this equipment been here and why wasn't it at the Superdome or the Convention Center, I wondered.

We kept walking, but were beginning to feel as if we were unwanted groupies chasing a rock star. Secretary Chertoff stopped for photo ops, gathering and smiling with other Homeland Security personnel on site, while barely acknowledging our presence. The Mayor was not asked to move in closer and the Secretary did not try to include him in his activities. We stood by and waited to see if the Secretary was going to work his way toward us for the scheduled meeting.

We had been following him about 30 minutes when the Mayor looked at me with an air of frustration and said, "Let's go."

"I agree, this stinks," I said, enraged that a federal official would be engaged in what seemed like childish game playing at a time like this. "It's so unprofessional – why would he schedule this meeting if his intent was to ignore us?"

"And look at all of the port-o-lets and equipment around here," the Mayor added. "If we had just had a couple of these lights in the city, it would have made a huge difference."

As if following a Homeland Security code of brotherhood, the Colonel said nothing.

As we got to the end of the road, the Secretary's entourage exited in several dark vehicles with tinted windows. Michael Brown stopped his car to get out and shake the Mayor's hand. "At least Brown is a gentleman," I told the Mayor later.

We arrived back at the Saints administration building and walked inside. In the cafeteria were sodas, fresh fruit, sandwiches and hand towels. Even though it was still morning, we sat down and enjoyed turkey sandwiches, ice-cold sodas and chips. Above us hung a sign coined for the Saints: "Gotta Have Faith."

After lunch, we crossed the Saints practice field to reach a long row of port-o-lets. Resembling a defensive lineman, Louis picked up a football on the field and tossed it to me. It felt good playing ball on an open field, forgetting about the worries in the city.

When the Mayor reappeared he said to me, "That's the first time I've used the bathroom in a week."

"That's TMI [too much information]," I replied.

Heading back, the Mayor, Colonel and I talked about the progress in the city. The previous day, General Honoré fulfilled his mission by moving at least 20,000 people out of the Convention Center in one day. The 17th Street Canal sandbagging was proceeding well with 85 percent of the breach now plugged. Troops had been arriving all day and the sense of lawlessness had nearly vanished.

The cavalry had finally arrived.

It was almost 11 a.m. when we landed back at the Dome.

"Oprah is next," I told the Mayor. I was excited because I had asked Press Secretary Tami to see if Oprah's producer could bring me a clean T-shirt and toiletries.

As we rounded the bend of the Dome, we saw a sea of reporters on the ramp. The closest one to us was CNN's Nic Robertson.

"Mayor, this story is big," I said. "Besides Christiane Amanpour, Nic Robertson is CNN's senior foreign correspondent." We stepped through the muck. With the limited access to communication, we were oblivious to the world outside of the city. "The rest of the country must be completely aware of what's happened."

Robertson put his microphone near the Mayor. "How many bodies are there?"

"I don't know, man, thousands," the Mayor replied. "I want to make sure these dead bodies get out of the water because mosquitoes are going to start to take effect. The larvaes are hatching as we speak. They're going to bite these dead people and they're going to spread diseases not only in Louisiana, but all over the South."

I wondered where the Mayor had gotten this theory of New Orleans mosquitoes spreading what, West Nile virus or malaria, throughout the South and made a note to verify it with Doc Stephens.

As Robertson pressed the Mayor for details about the response, the Mayor said, "I'm not going to forget the people who didn't act fast enough."

"Who are they?" Robertson asked.

"I'm not going to name names now," he replied.

Inside the Hyatt, I left the Mayor to find Oprah. On the plaza breezeway, a small crowd had gathered around her, including Chief Compass and Gralen Banks, the security director for the Hyatt, reflecting the icon's immense popularity. I introduced myself to Oprah and her producer, Lisa. Her whole team was dressed casually, including Oprah in a lime green shirt, blue jeans and rain boots.

As we walked to the atrium lobby, the cameras rolled as the Mayor and Chief Compass hugged Oprah and began to tell her their story. I stood back and watched as the interview unraveled into a very emotional scene. The Mayor began to tear up. Chief Compass, with hunched shoulders and shaking hands, also began to cry. Walking away from the set to collect his emotions, the Mayor eyeballed me. I walked over to him.

"Get him out of here right now," the Mayor whispered, not needing to tell me who "he" was.

I didn't know that Chief Compass had just told Oprah, "We've got babies being raped." But the Mayor had also chimed in, talking about "people in that frickin' Superdome for five days watching dead bodies, watching hooligans killing people, raping people." The Mayor and the Chief had indeed seen dead bodies, and who knew how many rapes had actually occurred, but these stories had not yet been substantiated.

Later, Marlon and I would have to defend the Chief and Mayor as criticism about their inaccuracies mounted.

"The Mayor was listening to officials, trusting that information they were providing was accurate," I would tell the reporters.

"It was a chaotic time in the city," Marlon would say. "Now that we've had time to reflect, we can say things were not the way they appeared."

Back with the television crew, I now had the unenviable task of keeping the Chief away from someone as loved as Oprah. I tried to corral him as the interview moved to the Dome, but he kept walking ahead, seemingly searching for the speck of lime green that was Oprah's bright shirt.

Walking next to Oprah, the Mayor expressed his lingering frustration. "The story that I think is going to be amazing to America is the amount of people that suffered. I just knew that this country, America — the richest country in the world — would not let Americans suffer," he said. "This state, with an $18 billion budget, how did they let their own people suffer like this? I just don't get it."

Nearing the Dome, I pulled Oprah's producer aside. "Did you bring the package?" I asked quietly.

"The what?" she responded, looking at me blankly.

"I had asked our press secretary Tami, to give you a message that I could really use a few basic necessities," I replied. "She must have forgotten to ask you." I turned my head and sighed, my hopes of toiletries and a clean shirt dashed completely.

The Mayor and Oprah stood at the entrance of the Dome. Oprah was insisting that the Mayor let her go inside, but the military did not want to let her in.

"I don't advise you to go in there," the Mayor said. I stood on the side with the Colonel as Chief Compass sidled back up to Oprah.

"I don't get it," Oprah said. "Thousands of people had to spend almost a week in here and I just want to go in and look. It's not fair that I can't even see it after they had to live in it."

"Sally, get over here," the Mayor hollered, urging me in closer. "Quit being so star struck."

"Star struck?" I said when I reached him. "I'm the only one not pressing into this group. She hardly has breathing room."

"She wants to go inside," he said. "What do you think?"

I knew his mind was already made up, but I nonetheless played along. "Whatever you think," I answered.

The Mayor made Oprah look at the camera and absolve the city of responsibility for whatever she might witness. Inside, the place was a wreck, but the views were far less dramatic than when evacuees had been living inside.

Leaving the Dome with Oprah and her crew, I saw Ted Koppel's producer, Mary Claude, walking toward me with an angry expression. "Oprah is now butting into our time," she said. "We're supposed to have the Mayor at 3p.m."

"We won't be much longer," I said.

"This is not right," Mary Claude snapped a few minutes later.

"Talk to Oprah's people if you have this big of a problem," I replied.

I realized too late that I shouldn't have said that. A few minutes later, a shouting match began between Oprah's producer, Lisa, and Koppel's producer, Mary Claude.

Lisa held her ground. "That woman's crazy!" she told me later. "I'm calling Ted Koppel."

Handling this major press event alone, I realized how frantic producers and reporters were to book the Mayor.

As we finished with Oprah, we followed Mary Claude to the "Nightline" set. The ABC crew had pitched a tent for the interview and I felt comfortable with the quality of show correspondent John Donvan's work.

Donvan began by asking the Mayor about his own house.

"I know it's gone," the Mayor answered. "I don't want to see it."

Why was the Mayor saying he was homeless, I wondered, when Greg had told us his house was fine?

"Tell me what you saw," Donvan asked.

"I went over to Charity Hospital, and all the windows blew out after the storm," he said. "They moved all the patients to the middle hallways. The doctors were running out of medicine and supplies."

I didn't know he had gone to Charity Hospital, but I was pleased he did. The medical professionals who sheltered our hospitals were performing heroic feats.

"I see the angel of death flying all over this city being allowed to roam and have a good time," the Mayor continued.

"I'm out at the highway last Thursday," Donvan said, "and Jesse Jackson comes in, looks at the scene, and says it looks like the scene from a slave ship. What's your response to that?"

"I will tell you this. I think it's, it could be, it's a class issue, for sure," the Mayor said. "I don't know if it's color or class."

I jotted a note to discuss the response to this question. Days later, the Mayor would tell reporter Gordon Russell of *The Times-Picayune*, "If it's race, fine, let's call a spade a spade, a diamond a diamond."

"In some way you think that New Orleans got second-class treatment?" Donvan asked.

"I can't explain the response," the Mayor said. "People got restless, and it was overcrowding at the Convention Center. We said, if you want to walk across the Crescent City Connection, there's buses coming, you may be able to find some relief. They started marching. At the parish line, the county line of Gretna, they were met with attack dogs and police officers with machine guns saying, 'you have to turn back because a looter got in the shopping center and set it afire, and we want to protect the property in this area.'"

"And what does that say to you?" Donvan asked.

"That says we're protecting property over human life," he said. "They weren't going to go in those doggone neighborhoods. Those people were looking to escape, and they cut off the last available exit route out of New Orleans."

After the interview, a reporter asked me for comment about Jefferson Parish President Aaron Broussard's alligator tears on "Meet the Press."

"I didn't see it, what happened?" I asked.

"He broke down and said 'no more press conferences'," the reporter replied.

"It sounds like he's repeating the Mayor," I replied.

Winding down in the Hyatt at the end of the day, Chief Compass shared news of another police incident. "There's been a shooting at the Danziger Bridge," he said. "Several people fired at some construction workers near the bridge, so we went out there. No officers were injured but we shot them."

It's about time, I shouted inside, not knowing that police may have inadvertently shot innocent bystanders, including a mentally disabled man. I breathed a huge sigh of relief knowing our residents were evacuated, the breach was almost closed, fires were burning out and the police had shot the bad guys.

On Sunday night, "60 Minutes" aired Scott Pelley's story exposing the Mayor's ungroomed face to the nation. Pelley asked the Mayor to explain how failed communications and dithering among agencies hurt the city.

"Too many people died because of lack of action, lack of coordination and some goofy laws that basically say there's not a clear distinction of when the federal government stops and when the state government starts," the Mayor said, referring to the Posse Comitatus Act.

"Bureaucracy?" Pelley asked.

"Bull–crap," the Mayor snapped. "When people are dying, bureaucracy should be thrown out of the water."

"You know what the national response authorities would say?" Pelley said. "That it's a disaster and hard to get stuff in there."

"Man, I don't want to hear any of that," the Mayor said. "This is a small city. It's about 500,000 people. We're not talking about taking over a country."

Gen. Russell Honoré (bad freaking John Wayne dude) arrived mid-week at the heliport in New Orleans, unfortunately without troops.

The National Guard slept on the ground as their choppers shielded them from the heat.

Makeshift beds made out of cardboard lined the ramps of the Dome.

The Mayor and Chief Compass listened as Dome evacuees cried out.

Leaving Air Force One, what could have been an historical moment, turned into a partisan battle.

Government leaders in charge when the power went out. From left, HUD Secretary Alphonso Jackson, Sen. Mary Landrieu, Mayor Nagin, FEMA Secretary Brown, President Bush, Governor Blanco, Sen. David Vitter, Homeland Security Secretary Michael Chertoff, Congressman William Jefferson, Congressman Bobby Jindal, Gen. Blum.

Dr. Brenda Hatfield and Colonel Terry Ebbert reunited while Andy Kopplin and Major General Bennett C. Landreneau conferred in the background.

The Mayor and General Blum would later become part of the media madness.

Mounds of trash and waste festered at the Superdome.

Late Saturday night, nearly a week after the storm, the last bus departed from the Convention Center.

Homeland Security Secretary Michael Chertoff, with FEMA Secretary Michael Brown, shook the Mayor's hand before virtually ignoring us.

At the New Orleans Saints training camp, bodyguard Louis instructed me to go out for a long pass.

Bodyguard Wondell Smith, TD, Sergeant Dazet, the Colonel, the Mayor, me and bodyguard Louis Martinez regrouped inside the Saints cafeteria.

With Oprah at the Dome, moments before entering the stadium.

The Mayor and General Honore in the back of a Humvee.

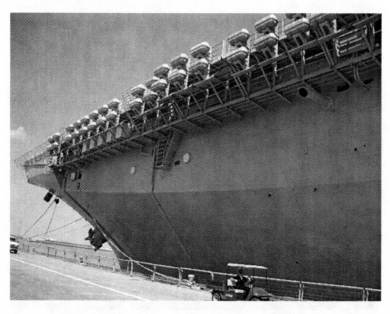

The USS Iwo Jima, where I slept like a baby.

Our new and expanded press corps.

With the dynamic "Mork and Mindy" (Lt. Col. Mike Pierson and Maj. Mindy Morgan of the 82nd Airborne), in the emergency center.

The Governor invited the Mayor to lunch to partner on rebuilding the city, but their relationship stayed fractured in part due to the Mayor's earlier endorsement of Bobby Jindal in the 2003 Governor's race.

Chapter 11

Conspiracy Theories

Monday, September 5

I awakened knowing the city would never be the same. Phones didn't work, there was no electricity or sanitation and most of our residents were now in cities all over America. The home of Oysters Rockefeller and red beans and rice is now rancid, I thought. Thinking of food, I crawled out of bed and became sick again.

On the fourth floor, I could feel that tensions had subsided as the Mayor and Greg joked in a macho, self-confident manner.

"I've got shit happening on the sixth floor now," Greg said. "We're rockin'."

"You the man," the Mayor told him.

The Mayor agreed to another interview with Matt Lauer on the "Today" show, hoping to avoid a repeat with Campbell Brown. "Mayor Nagin, good morning to you," Lauer began. "One of the questions I've been wanting to ask you over the last several days and I haven't heard an answer for this, all of those people that were told to go to the Convention Center, some 15,000 people, told help would be there and help didn't arrive for days. Do you have an answer as to who told them to go there?"

As I listened in the headset, I watched the Mayor's demeanor closely as he wiped his sweaty brow.

"We started looking around the city to see what other locations were dry. And the Convention Center was one, and the Police Department went over there and opened it up."

That interview was easier, I thought. Maybe we will survive this after all.

We headed toward the Dome. Dateline's Stone Phillips joined us at the heliport for a flyover. The rooftops had cleared as Coast Guard helicopters blanketed the sky. "Mayor, where does the city stand?" Phillips asked.

"I see a light at the end of the tunnel," he answered.

"Federal officials, including Homeland Security Secretary Chertoff, have said that the only way to have avoided this catastrophe was to have evacuated better, earlier, and that falls to state and local officials," Phillips said. "Your response?"

"I think the spinmeisters are in full effect," the Mayor answered. "I will tell you, we as a nation failed a group of people that needed it the most."

We rounded the corner after the flyover. Soledad O'Brien from CNN walked over. "Hi, I'm Soledad."

"I'm Sally," I answered.

"Oh, you're Sally," she said, shaking hands. "I was told to look for you. Can I have the Mayor?"

"Catch him right now as we walk," I answered. Because he was hard to pin down, I would say this often in the weeks to come. She hurried next to the Mayor and put the microphone near his face as they navigated around piles of trash.

"Mayor Nagin, there are people who say your evacuation plan, obviously in hindsight, was disastrous," Soledad said.

"Let me ask you this question," the Mayor said. "When you have a city of 500,000 people, and you have a Category 5 storm bearing down on you, and the best you've ever done is evacuate 60 percent of the people out of the city, and you have never issued a mandatory evacuation in the city's history, a city that is a couple of hundred years old, I did that," he said, highlighting the mandatory evacuation's success in pushing out over 80 percent of the city. "And as a last resort, sent people to the Superdome as a shelter of last resort. When that filled up, we sent them to the Convention Center. Now, you tell me what else we could have done?"

Soledad kept the microphone near his mouth, working hard to keep in step with the much taller Mayor.

"And what the state was doing, I don't frigging know," the Mayor added. "But I tell you, I am pissed. It wasn't adequate." I gave the Mayor a cut signal, but he ignored my cue. "She said she needed 24 hours to make a decision," he said. "And more people died."

Already a problem before the storm, the Mayor's trust level was now running below zero as he began to mull over rumor-driven stories of people circumventing his authority, tent cities being planned and contracts being sought.

In one such instance, a rumor had been circulating that a bomb caused the Lower Ninth Ward levee breach. Unfortunately, this rumor had some historical precedent. In 1927, bombs were detonated in levees in the lower section of the city to spare the historical and wealthier sections from flooding. But the Mayor had received details from engineers as to how this breach had occurred and it was clearly not a bomb. One month after the storm, the Reverend Louis Farrakhan ignited the rumor when he said the Mayor told him "about a 25-foot crater located under the levee break."

"Mayor, you and I sat with General Crear from the Corps of Engineers as he explained the barge and the failure of the levee walls." I had said.

Army Brigadier General Robert Crear, an African American engineer, had described the burst of Katrina's storm surge coming in like a funnel through the Mississippi River Gulf Outlet into the Industrial Canal.

"Do you really believe the levee was bombed?" I asked the Mayor.

"No," he answered.

"Then you must say that publicly to stop the suspicion," I pleaded.

He eventually did.

In another case, discussions with Water Board Director Marcia St. Martin convinced the Mayor that workers in Jefferson Parish had closed the section of the canal lock called the Hoey's Cut right before Katrina to protect Jefferson Parish at the expense of New Orleans. "Send this information to Ed Bradley at '60 Minutes'," he instructed.

I asked Marcia for her opinion. "Do you believe the Hoey Cut was purposefully closed to keep Jefferson Parish dry at the expense of New Orleans?" I asked.

"No," she said. But the Mayor was convinced otherwise and sent the pictures to Ed Bradley anyway. The famed "60 Minutes" correspondent did not respond.

Later, I saw an interesting report that I shared with the Mayor. "NBC's Lisa Myers did a piece on why blacks tend to believe urban legends and conspiracy theories so readily," I said. "I now understand you a lot better."

He laughed.

Halfway expecting it, I received a call later that day from Andy Kopplin, the Governor's chief of staff. "Sally, it's Andy. Is it true the Mayor said that more people died because of the Governor?"

"No," I answered too quickly before correcting myself. "What he was trying to say was that we needed action quickly and that hold ups caused more problems."

Andy was clearly distressed.

"We watched the interview, Sally," he said. "We heard him say it."

"I was there and his intent was not to say that the Governor made people die, but that our frustration was with the bureaucracy," I said.

We hung up and I looked for the Mayor. "You need to watch how you say that more people died due to the Governor's slow response," I advised.

"Screw them," he said, not wanting to be scolded. "I'm going to continue to tell the truth as I see it."

I worried that Coach Blanco would come down and bust his ass.

The Mayor agreed to let Diane Sawyer sit in on one of our meetings at the Hyatt. Dressed in casual clothes, her trademark blonde hair was coiffed and shiny. After the meeting, she asked the Mayor, "Do you have a sense the White House is now moving to make state and local officials the target?

"The target of what?" he asked.

"Responsibility," she answered. I listened intently. A White House smear campaign would hurt our recovery and I needed to be as ready as possible if one came into play.

"Do you think the President delayed because he didn't have enough information or do you think he didn't have the right instinct?" Sawyer asked.

"I think the President was suffering from the same thing I was suffering from initially. I would ask questions. They would tell me what was supposed to happen. I would follow up to find out what really happened. And it wasn't happening," the Mayor said. "And I don't think the right information got to the President."

I walked over to City Hall to see how the stalwarts in the emergency center were faring. Chief Matthews sat stationed in the same place he had been for over a week, his bifocals still perched on his worn out face. The Colonel appeared with comrades in tow.

"You know, a lot of these people would have drowned if we hadn't had the Dome," he said. "It was filthy and hot, but there was order."

The picture of what had transpired in the Dome would become clear later as the Police Department confirmed that, despite comments made by the Mayor and Chief Compass, the number of violent acts appeared limited: an attempted assault on a young woman in a rest room, the shooting of a National Guardsman which appeared to be an accident, one suicide and no documented homicides. Only two of the 14 bodies inside the Dome had gunshot wounds, far fewer than we had first been told. In spite of the suffering, the Colonel was right: the Dome had been a fairly secure environment.

"Man," the Mayor would later say, "even brothers from the 'hood organized to protect women and children from the addicts and thugs."

Later that evening, Secretary Chertoff and General Honoré came to the Entergy command post to meet with the Mayor. They informed the Mayor that the President had been in Baton Rouge meeting with the Governor.

Observing Secretary Chertoff more closely, I noticed his angular jaw and devil's beard promoted a sinister apperance. As the person responsible for protecting the United States from Osama Bin Laden, Chertoff had to be accomplished, but I wondered how a person in this high of a position could have stumbled so greatly during the emergency response. Perhaps he knew how to keep terrorists from striking on our soil, but didn't completely understand domestic emergency response.

General Honoré reported on the progress of evacuation. "We've finished the Dome and Convention Center areas and are working all throughout the city now," he said.

As we wrapped up, Secretary Chertoff addressed the Mayor. "The President would like to speak to you." All of the aides departed the room while the Mayor, General Honoré, the Secretary and I dialed the President on the speakerphone.

"Mayor, I'm sorry I wasn't able to get you today," began the President on the Entergy speakerphone. "I came to Baton Rouge today and didn't even see you. They couldn't reach you and I feel badly about that."

"That's OK, Mr. President," the Mayor replied.

"How are things?"

"Things are definitely better."

"Have you seen the work at the 17th Street Canal?" the President asked, referring to the work of the U.S. Army Corps of Engineers to plug the levee breaches.

"Yes sir, and it looks good, thank you."

"Good."

"Mr. President," added the Mayor, "I need to tell you that I think you did something right in Texas. The people there have been incredible. If you could let the governor of Texas know how much I appreciate that."

"I will call Governor Perry and tell him," the President continued. "Is there anything else we can do?"

"Yes, we need a lot of help de-watering the city. If you could focus on making that happen, that would be great," the Mayor asked. Once we plugged the levees, our pumping stations could hopefully drain the water and make the city livable again.

"We can do that," the President said.

When the call ended, I pressed the button to hang up the phone. Secretary Chertoff and General Honoré had sat by quietly to give the Mayor and the President time to speak.

"Mayor, anything else?" General Honoré asked.

I suggested to the Mayor that he discuss the late night meeting we had had with FEMA, in which they talked about eliminating food and water distribution.

"Yes," the Mayor informed the Secretary. "We met with FEMA officials and they told us that if we enforce the mandatory evacuation, they will no longer be able to provide food and water in the city."

"Fuck that," shouted Secretary Chertoff, "that's not going to happen."

This guy gave me the heebie-jeebies, but I welcomed his support.

Upon leaving, General Honoré invited us to sleep on the USS Iwo Jima, an amphibious assault ship stationed at our Port. I gratefully accepted.

Outside, the muggy air was gray as General Honoré arrived in his military Humvee to pick us up. We headed toward the Mississippi River through the ruined city, its buildings now etched in darkness. As we reached the wharf, a towering structure loomed overhead, too big for a city as quaint as New Orleans. It was the USS Iwo Jima.

I boarded the ship as a massive helicopter stood ready on the deck. The sheer length and soaring height of the massive vessel confirmed for me the absolute strength of the American military, and I wished they had been nearer in the threatening first five days.

A female sailor was assigned to assist me on board. "I will show you to your cabin before taking you down to the medical quarters," she said.

I dreaded the upcoming physical and psychological examination that I was told I would have to take.

"I'm totally fine, just a little nauseated each day," I told the ship's doctor. "The only thing I'm worried about is this rash all over my body." I showed him my splotchy stomach.

"That's dysentery," he replied. "We'll get you a tetanus shot and you should be fine. I walked back to my room and took a much-needed shower in a 2'x2' stall.

Dinner in the Captain's quarters that evening reminded me of Sunday meals at my grandmother's house: roast beef, mashed potatoes and peas. I gobbled it up.

After dinner, I tried to use my phone. Our Blackberries worked sporadically on the downstairs deck. I climbed up and down the companionway ladders, holding on tightly to the wires on the rigging. Messages came in rapidly down below.

NBC producer Matt Zimmerman asked for another "Today" show interview. "Katie will be on Canal Street at 5:15 a.m.," Mr. Persistence said.

I knew the Mayor would not agree to wake up that early so I declined. Matt pleaded. "What about Ann Curry? She is also on the ship." I declined again.

"OK, let's work out a better time and place for Katie," Matt said. Sick of hearing me talk about it, the Mayor agreed to meet them at 6:00 the next morning on Canal Street.

A seaman took me on a tour of the vessel. In the media quarters, I met Ann Curry and immediately regretted that she was not conducting the Mayor's interview. She was bright and knowledgeable.

And she was here.

Chapter 12

The Media Circus

Tuesday, September 6

At 5 a.m., my devoted sailor provided my reveille. "You have guests here," she said, knocking lightly. I wearily stepped out of the cabin and saw Matt and another producer, Sarah Clagett, from the "Today" show in the hall.

"It's getting late and the Mayor is supposed to be on our set by now," Sarah said. "We've been knocking on his door but there's no answer."

"I'm sorry, I overslept," I said.

I walked down the hallway to the Mayor's quarters. "Mayor, wake up," I hollered. I didn't get a response so I opened the door and entered the sitting room. "Mayor, come on," I said, knocking on the door to his bedroom. Not a peep. "Mayor, you have to get up. The people from the 'Today' show are here waiting for you." I hesitantly opened the door while turning my head.

"What?" he said bouncing up.

"It's me, we agreed to do media this morning."

"OK, I'm up," he replied.

I walked down the hall to wake up Louis and Wondell. The Mayor came out of his room wearing a yellow polo shirt emblazoned with the logo of the USS Iwo Jima. The shirt was crisp, making him appear healthier.

"You're a trouper," I told him.

We ran down the galleys and drove away from the wharf in Big Daddy. On Canal Street, known as one of America's widest main streets, media trailers packed the neutral ground. I hopped out of the car and walked over to the NBC set.

"The Mayor is ready when you are and he'll be waiting in the car," I told Matt. It was still dark outside. I crossed the street to look at a building that had burned down, wondering if it was the one recently renovated by my friends Joy and Boysie Bollinger. Seeing it wasn't, I walked back to the car.

Soon, the producers flagged us over and we walked onto the set. As the Mayor waited to be miked, a new phone that Greg the techie had given me rang. "Hello?" I said.

"Sally, this is Kathleen Blanco."

"Good morning, Governor," I said, waving my hand at the Mayor. "Mayor," I mouthed, "it's the Governor." He shook his head *no* as he prepared to go on.

"Sally, I need to talk to the Mayor," she began.

"Governor, I'm sorry," I told her as I moved away from the set. "He's not available right now."

"Well, this is important, I need to talk to him about what's going on," she said. "Right now, the National Guard is doing a good job and they are the ones that should be in charge."

"OK," I responded, jotting down her comments.

"The feds sent General Honoré here without resources," she said firmly. "This needs to be a joint command, not federalized." I could see where this conversation was headed: another partisan battle of who should be doing what.

The Governor's voice grew louder. "These are the facts," she said sternly, "and the Mayor needs to not speak about what he knows not of." I wrote quickly as she became more irate. "If the Mayor wants to go toe to toe, I will go toe to toe with him," she continued. "The White House is playing politics with this because the President hated the criticism. The military does not have police power and nothing is preventing them from coming in and doing what they need to do." Her voice began to crack.

"I'm listening," I assured her. I looked at the Mayor and mimed tears coming down my face as if to say, *She's crying.*

He shook his head again to let me know he did not want the phone.

"While we were saving lives, they were talking about federalizing," the Governor continued. It was obvious the Governor was under tremendous strain, but she was now allowing partisanship to become a problem for her and the recovery.

As her tears began to flow, the phone call disconnected.

"Thank you, Jesus," I said. The last thing I was prepared to do this early in the morning was speak to a crying governor.

Katie had not yet appeared so I walked back over to the Mayor on the set. "I'll fill you in after the interview," I said, "but the Governor is upset and doesn't want this to become the state versus you and the President."

"To hell with the state," vented the Mayor. "They withheld resources."

In my mind, the Governor had to be working as hard as the Mayor to do the right thing, but the Mayor felt like she was working against him.

Katie Couric moved into position and conducted the interview. "Mayor Nagin, do you think there are a lot of people still in their homes after all this time still alive?"

"Yeah. They're pulling them out," the Mayor answered. "You've got that and you have people here who are saying 'I don't want to leave'."

"Many Americans have been dismayed and shocked to see so many people who are living in impoverished conditions. Nine percent of the people of this nation live below the poverty line. In New Orleans, it's 28 percent," Couric said.

"Well, you know, it's definitely put a different face and spin on the way we live and the class situations and I know there's all kind of racial discussions going on," he replied.

I made a note. It was about time we accounted for our failure as a city to have allowed such horrific poverty levels and a pitiful educational system to exist for such a long time.

"Let's go to Harrah's," the Mayor said when we finished. Police operations were now stationed at the shuttered casino and he wanted to thank members of the force.

The Mayor made his way through the small groups of officers gathered outside. After shaking hands and patting backs, Deputy Chief Riley, the Mayor and I sat inside Big Daddy. Squashed between them, I listened intently as my body lurched forward. Like a symphony conductor, Chief Riley was already organizing a census and assessing the city's security.

On the ride back, we decided to call a press conference to announce the plans the Mayor had created for first responders.

"Also, you need to remind people that we will be enforcing the mandatory evacuation," I said. Since the water was only safe for bathing if it was boiled and looting and criminal activity continued, the Mayor issued a new emergency order to this effect.

That afternoon, we held our first official press conference since the storm. Thankfully, Audrey was now able to e-mail talking points to the Mayor. "My thanks goes out to many, many people, both that stood on the ground with us when we were battling to keep this city together," the Mayor said. "The resources are now here in the city of New Orleans and we need to get this job done and complete it," he said.

The press conference produced several more questions: "How many cubic yards of garbage is there?" "When will postal service resume?" and "How do you feel about Congress authorizing CDL loans instead of grants under the Stafford Act?

I had always prided myself on knowing a little about a lot, but the onslaught of questions left me feeling like a struggling student.

Before the storm, with a revolving press corps of about 50 people that included print, radio and TV, our media pool represented mostly local outlets. Regional and national coverage occurred mainly during storm season. Because the Mayor was a charismatic figure, we occasionally received requests for profiles. Three weeks after the storm, a rough count showed over 1,000 media and documentary personnel in town. Crews arrived from countries all over the world and each of the major networks established bureaus in the city.

For months I carried five cell phones, although none was guaranteed to work. When my Blackberry did work, the voice-mail that accepted 30 messages would fill up within an hour. I drove my car with my knee on the wheel and two hands on the phones.

George Stephanopoulos summed up my status then quite succinctly when I told him I felt a bit like he must have after Bill Clinton became president. "Sounds like your current job is more challenging than WH [White House]," he replied.

The media requests during those months were rampant and often included calls from the hosts themselves. "Sally, this is Matt Lauer," the message said, "hoping to get a chance to talk to you and the Mayor."

The requests generally included needing the Mayor in a unique setting. "I want him walking and talking in the Lower Ninth Ward," or "If I can just have him riding in a military vehicle," or even, "If we can get him inside the Superdome near the dead bodies, that would be great."

We restricted his appearances to press conferences in an effort to accommodate as many requests as possible. The Mayor hated too much media pressure and would snap at me when the queries became widespread. "Calm these reporters down," he said.

I initially worked with producers on network requests and was impressed with Gail Chalef at CNN, Ariane Nalty at ABC and Matt Zimmerman at NBC. Frequently under the gun, producers and reporters sometimes competed within their own organization to secure the Mayor.

One day I received a call from a producer who accused me of being racist for not granting an exclusive to Jason Carroll, whom the producer identified as the senior African American reporter at CNN. I asked the caller for his name and hung up the phone.

I called CNN's Ken Tucker to report the affront. "Ken, you guys are shooting yourself in the foot. You have a producer for a reporter on Paula Zahn's show crying racism, Aaron Brown's producers are trying to get us to not appear on Larry King and the morning show producers are telling me that we need to do the morning show instead of evening shows practically every day."

Ken called later to say that the president of CNN put out an e-mail to try to correct the problems.

Competition among the national morning shows was by far the stiffest. One morning I booked the "Today" show at 7 a.m. and "Good Morning America" at 7:30 a.m. GMA producers called me several times trying to change the time slot they had for the Mayor. One of the producers called in tears.

"Diane [Sawyer] is so upset about this. She even said, 'I thought the Mayor liked me'," the producer implored.

"What on earth are you talking about?" I asked.

"Sally, you've given us the 7:30 slot. That's not even news!" she said, indicating what a loss the show would suffer if we appeared in any slot other than 6 a.m. Eastern.

"Look, we've already booked it and it's too late in the evening to make the change," I replied.

"Why are you doing this to us?" cried the producer. "What did we do to you?"

Like network producers, I also felt the pressure. After announcing an afternoon press conference about which we could not release the details, Laura Parker of *USA Today* and Cece Connelly of *The Washington Post* chewed me out. "You cannot call a press conference and not tell us what it's about," they said when I arrived at the Sheraton Hotel, where the announcement would be made. "We have to decide if it's more important than another event we're trying to cover."

"I simply cannot share the information yet," I said.

"This is not how you do it, Sally," they said before storming off.

In the international press corps, the Mayor was sought after primarily because of his strong comments about President Bush in the Garland Robinette interview. With dozens of international reporters in town, many were eager for additional comments about President Bush.

Requests also came in from entertainment shows, which were easier to decline. This was a crisis, not something to joke about with Jay Leno on the "Tonight Show."

Even the locals needed more than I was able to give. "We need some one-on-one time with the Mayor," one reporter from a flooded station said. "You cannot forget the locals, Sally."

"But you're not even on the air," I replied.

Beverly McKenna, an African American newspaper publisher, accused me of giving an exclusive to *The Times-Picayune* when a committee of the Mayor's rebuilding commission used their own public relations firm to announce their plans. "So you're giving an exclusive to an all-white paper while leaving us out?" she asked.

"Beverly, I had nothing to do with that story," I replied. "That committee handles its own communications." Nothing I could say would rid her of the chip she carried on her shoulder.

Most reporters were eager and adventurous, like Susan Roesgen, who climbed 27 flights to see if she could find the Mayor. Some, however, looked for direction. Susan Roberts of CBS, a former New Orleans reporter, called when she landed. "Hi Sally, it's Susan Roberts," she said. "Do you have any story ideas?"

"Unfortunately, this is reporters' heaven," I replied. "You will have no problem finding stories."

From my days as a journalism student, I had always admired great reporting. Months into the aftermath, I became greatly impressed with the work of Corey Dade of *The Wall St. Journal,* Cathy Booth Thomas of *TIME,* John Roberts, formerly of CBS and now CNN, Martin Savidge of NBC and Dan Baum of *The New Yorker.* The BBC, *Newsweek,* ABC's "Nightline," *The Washington Post* and Bloomberg were heavily invested in the story, but few matched the commitment of *The*

New York Times and anchors Anderson Cooper and Brian Williams in keeping the story alive.

The nightly reporting of Cooper and Williams became a glue that bound together many communities in Louisiana, Mississippi and Alabama. Unfortunately, our experience with both of these reporters was not ideal.

The Mayor gave an interview to Anderson Cooper one evening, which I did not attend. Afterwards, he complained about the interview.

"What happened?" I asked.

The Mayor would not elaborate but did not want to interview with Anderson Cooper again.

As Cooper came back to town, his producers tried repeatedly to schedule an interview. "You should do this, he's moved into Aaron Brown's spot at night," I said. "And his audience grew 41 percent among 25-54 year olds during Katrina."

Because of the Mayor's reluctance, I pushed confirmed dates back on several occasions. Eventually, we firmed up a time for Anderson Cooper that would follow a scheduled Spike Lee interview. When the Spike Lee interview concluded, the Mayor decided that he wanted to stroll through the French Quarter with Spike Lee. I reminded him of his commitment.

"I'm not going to that interview," he said.

"You cannot just cancel Anderson Cooper," I said.

"Watch me," he said.

When a second interview finally occurred, Cooper was polite and the Mayor handled the queries with ease.

My handling of Brian Williams was unprofessional. In preparation, I met Williams and his NBC crew at the Sheraton Hotel and asked way too many questions about the set up and location of the interview, handling the Mayor like the manager of a rock star rather than his communications director. Williams later wrote in his blog that it felt like the Mayor had too much P.R. around.

> One of the revelations of yesterday for our traveling team was our first exposure to Mayor Ray Nagin. The single most striking aspect of meeting the mayor was what had to happen BEFORE we were allowed to meet the mayor. He has apparently hired a P.R. team of loyalists who could easily protect the White House. And by that I mean: the house, its occupants and all 18 acres. In fact, someone in our group remarked (and mind you: this is an interview on the second floor "atrium level" of the downtown Sheraton) that we've conducted interviews with Presidents of the United States with less discussion of camera angles, walking distances, duration, lighting and timing.

I wondered now how CNN's Howard Kurtz would dissect the media coverage regarding Katrina on "Reliable Sources."

Thumbs up, I imagined.

Later that day, the Mayor pulled me aside to tell me that the Police Department was about to be painted as corrupt and that the situation with Chief Compass had become worse. "We are losing credibility whenever he's on the air," he said.

"I know." It was an obvious problem that anyone looking closely could see.

"Shut him down, Sally, or he's out," the Mayor said. Keeping him off the air would be a difficult task and I decided to talk to Marlon since he was always positioned like a good scout at the Chief's side.

"Marlon, the Mayor does not want the Chief doing one more interview and he has told me to reel him in immediately," I said.

"This is bad," Marlon sighed.

"I need your help," I confessed.

"Sally," he replied, "I can't be the heavy here. I'm a cop and he's my boss. I cannot go against his orders."

"Do you want my job?" I asked.

"No, I love being a cop and this could mess it up for me," he said.

"I understand," I told him. He had been through so much tragedy, including the loss of Paul. "I'll handle it myself."

Marlon helped me with strategy. "I'm going to bump all media requests to you. It will not work for me to say no to reporters in front of the Chief." I agreed to take the calls. I now had to muzzle another person besides Greg but this time it was a guy with a gun who seemed more fragile by the minute.

Suddenly, my phones were on fire with questions and confusion. "The Chief said we need your approval to talk to him. What's going on here?" reporters asked.

Every time I declined a media request for the Chief, my telephone rang. "This is stupid that I can't talk," Compass would scream. "Why are you doing this? It's worse not speaking to these people – they think something is up."

I was caught in a delicate situation and urged the Mayor to talk directly to the Chief.

"Not yet," he said.

Chapter 13

Stuck on Stupid

September and Beyond

It felt like a lifetime since I had seen my family and I woke up excited knowing I finally would. For now, we would be able to stay in Baton Rouge with the Reilly family, who were generously opening their home to many refugees. Ron had picked up Cassidy and McClain and enrolled them in a new school in Baton Rouge.

The Mayor was heading to Dallas to see his family and many of our first responders would also soon be reunited with their families, thanks to teams of backup reinforcements now flowing in the city.

"Dang it," I said as I looked at four locked doors on Ron's car at the Audubon Zoo. I had gotten dropped off here to drive his car to Baton Rouge, since he had already taken mine out of the city. "Where's the freaking key?"

Since Ron had forgotten to leave a key and mine were nowhere to be found, I went inside the zoo to see if I could borrow a car from someone there. Dan Maloney, the general curator who had so vigilantly watched over the animals during the storm, handed me the keys to a beat-up old van. I hit the road, but barely.

I turned off my phones to listen to the news on the radio. The first story highlighted a $51 billion supplemental request in Congress for Katrina relief. I wondered how we would spend $51 billion with a city budget of only $700 million, but nonetheless I was thrilled that money would soon be flowing into the city.

I turned on CNN and listened to a reporter describe our implementation of forced evacuations in the city:

> So far, no signs the evacuation order is being carried out just yet, but expect it to get underway the next few hours, certainly during the course of today. It's not really clear exactly how this evacuation, this forced evacuation, will be carried out. What Mayor Ray Nagin has said is that all people must now leave the city whether they like it or not and whether they are on their own private property or not. But talking with the National Guard and members of the 82nd Airborne Division that we were out with yesterday, they said they've not received any clear instructions on how to go about it.

I made a note to talk to the Mayor about our effectiveness. Now more than ever City Hall needed good organization, with talented people executing fully developed plans, something our office had lacked in the past. Through the years, several people had urged the Mayor to get a chief of staff, but he worried about putting too much control in the hands of one person. Now there was enough work for a hundred chiefs of staff.

I had not driven far in the van when Rush Limbaugh started talking about New Orleans. "The Mayor of New Orleans did not even follow his own emergency plan," Limbaugh said, obviously holding a copy of our emergency evacuation plan. "This document talks all about evacuating people with buses, but the Mayor of New Orleans did not evacuate residents with his buses."

Great, I thought, just what we needed.

"The Mayor also did not go inside the Dome," Rush said.

"Yes he did!" I shouted at the radio. "We did go inside the Dome, just not a lot."

Rush concluded by talking about Louisiana's legacy of corruption. "That's our past!" I screamed, hoping indeed it was our past. I wondered if this was the White House's targeted campaign to discredit us to which Diane Sawyer had referred.

Flipping back to CNN radio, I heard Pentagon correspondent Jamie McIntyre reporting on the New Orleans Police Department. "Sources at the Pentagon said only 500 police officers stayed in New Orleans and that the other two-thirds abandoned their posts." I called CNN immediately, this time getting through.

"Mr. McIntyre," I said. "You erroneously reported that only 500 officers stayed in the city. That is not the case at all."

"That's what I was told," he said.

"Can you please tell me where you got this?" I asked. "I'm familiar with your work and find it very credible, but a thousand officers simply did not leave."

He told me he would check his source and get right back to me. When he called back, he quoted the source as Lieutenant General Steven Blum, chief of the National Guard. General Blum, who had spoken to the Mayor on Air Force One, told CNN that the Mayor had provided him with that information. I informed the reporter that a wire had been crossed because the Mayor knew this was not true.

On FOX News, Tony Snow reported that one-third of our police officers were simply phantom cops. I called his producers and demanded that they retract the story and share the source. Unfortunately, the story came from a blog that had started the rumor and Snow had run with it.

Tuning back in to the radio, a report came on claiming that four people in New Orleans had been infected with Vibrio vulnificus. Coroner Dr. Frank Minyard said we would never know how many bodies had washed out to sea and reports of cholera, typhoid and hepatitis had begun to surface. But Vibrio vulnificus, what was that?

This was Crisis Communications 101.

Communications experts Mark Romig and Margaret Beer would later come to the city to assist with rumor control and crisis communications. Margaret drafted a proposal to FEMA to fund the crisis plan, which included the creation of a media center and advertising in major cities throughout the United States to reach evacuees. Granted preliminary approval by FEMA, the proposal was sent over the course of a few months to several FEMA parties for approval. Each time, the proposal was kicked back for modification, including one rejection where only two words needed changing.

The final proposal was never approved.

A major faux pas occurred a few months after the hurricane when the President visited New Orleans, this time to meet with small business owners affected by the storm. I asked the Mayor if Alberta Pate, our Housing Director, could attend since she was a Republican who admired the President. Instead, the Mayor instructed me to ask the White House for a seat for Greg the techie. In the meeting, Greg and I both sat in chairs along the wall while the President held a roundtable regarding the problems facing businesses. As the meeting ended, Steve Perry,

President of the New Orleans Convention and Visitors Bureau, urged the President to send the message that New Orleans was now OK.

But instead of the President's message, the press heard from Greg the techie, who gave an unauthorized interview to CNN.

CNN's Susan Roesgen reported that, "Meffert says he explained the problem to President Bush today and the president commiserated but didn't offer any way to cut the red tape."

Good grief, I sighed. Greg was claiming he explained the problems to the President, but Greg had not even spoken to the President.

An e-mail arrived from Maggie Grant at the White House. "Unfortunate coverage of the fellow from your office that we included in the meeting to watch," she said. "We live to fight and work another day."

"Damn. I am so sorry, he can be a real loose cannon," I replied, regretting greatly that this had occurred. "I'm awfully sorry – that is my job."

I alerted the Mayor about Greg's interview, and he snapped back at me.

"When he [Greg] has a success with the media he is most dangerous because he will get very flip," he said, referring to Greg's recent *Wall Street Journal* front-page story. "He also needs to stop saying he speaks for me."

Greg knew the expectations of interviews: Start on time, keep it short, be respectful but keep your answers honest and concise, never go off the record and do not speak for anyone else. With this bombshell interview, he somehow managed to break almost every rule.

A few weeks later during a press conference with federal and state officials, General Honoré, aka John Wayne, admonished me about the chaotic messages we were delivering to the public. "You have to get the press to do their job," he said firmly. "They are not reporting on what's important and it's confusing the public."

I listened respectfully as he spoke sternly in my ear.

"There's public information that people are depending on the government to put out," he continued. "Everyone that's part of the public message needs to know this so we don't confuse the public."

General Honoré was right. Between my lack of planning for the loss of power, the repeating of unsubstantiated rumors, the Mayor's rants, Greg's ego and Chief Compass' breakdowns, we were doing a terrible job of keeping the public informed.

When it was General Honoré's turn at the microphone, he railed at the press, "Don't get stuck on stupid, people."

After driving an hour on the Interstate in the dilapidated van, I pulled into the winding driveway at Winifred and Kevin Reilly's home in Baton Rouge. Cassidy and McClain ran out to meet me and gave me the warmest hug I had ever received. We held on tight for several minutes as tears filled my eyes.

"Mom, my birthday is Sunday," McClain said. "Have you gotten a present for me yet?" As young teenagers, they longed for the world they knew to return.

"Not yet, sweetie," I replied, "but I promise I will."

Ron came out and hugged me, too. It had been a long journey for everyone.

While the Mayor visited his family in Dallas, members of the Executive Staff that were now in New Orleans called a press conference on the steps of City Hall. Still hugging my children, I turned on the giant screen television in the Reilly's den, which now served as our new bedroom. Chief Compass stood at the podium as CNN and MSNBC carried the press conference live.

"First of all, I want to take a personal moment," Compass said, addressing the crowd. "My wife is eight months pregnant. And the doctor that's performing the delivery of my wife is in Denham Springs. Her name is Dr. B-E-N-A-N-T-I, Dr. Benanti. And she's very distraught and upset because she cannot find her uncle," he said.

I held on tight to the children as I braced myself.

"So if anyone knows the whereabouts of Peter K-U-Y-P – it's pronounced 'Kipe'," Chief Compass continued his confusing plea, "please call Dr. Benanti."

Representing the city on national television, Chief Compass had actually spelled his wife's gynecologist's name to help find a lost uncle whose name he also spelled.

"The reason I remain so composed over the entire deal is because the people in Denham Springs are taking care of my family and my wife and my child," Compass said. "And the people at the Ritz Carlton are taking care of my daughters from a previous marriage."

"Holy moly, mother of glory," I screamed. Now the Chief was on national television talking about his children from a previous marriage. I ran to my Blackberry to send an e-mail to the Colonel to pull him away from the podium.

"Today, I want to let you know that we've made over 200 arrests as of now," Compass said, finally getting down to business. "There are vicious rumors about children being found dead inside the Convention Center. We have swept the entire Convention Center. There are no children found there. And we have no confirmed reports of any type of sexual assaults."

"Chief, this would be the perfect time to apologize for perpetuating those rumors," I said out loud, still hoping he would step away.

"Mom, quit talking to the TV," Cassidy said.

Sherry finally stepped up to the mike and relieved my approaching migraine.

"I'm Sherry Landry, city attorney for New Orleans, and I'm here to address you only on issues related to the mandatory evacuation," she said. "At this time, force is not being used to evacuate those persons who are already in the city. Rather, our officers and troops continue to *strongly encourage* those folks in the city that are not associated with the recovery effort to leave, for their safety and for the safety of our officers, troops and contractors."

While Sherry spoke about the lack of force, video of law enforcement using a battering ram to get inside a home ran alongside her.

When the press conference finally ended, I let out a long exhale. "It's finally over!" The floodwaters would soon be departing our city, leaving behind destroyed lives, pets, cars and homes, but people, including fragile Chief Compass and loose-cannon Greg, would soon be reuniting with their families.

My Blackberry buzzed. I left the kids for a minute and walked out on a deck in Winifred and Kevin's expansive yard filled with Louisiana cypress and magnolias trees, azaleas, camellias, iris and lizard tails. After taking in every inch of the uninhibited natural surroundings, I looked at my e-mail. Michael Brown had resigned his position at FEMA and Coast Guard Vice Admiral Thad Allen had been named head of the Katrina relief efforts.

I sat on a bench and breathed deeply in the beautiful oasis.

The following Saturday evening, two weeks after Katrina's fury had ripped New Orleans to shreds, I sat nervously on the same deck. All through the night, I tried to convince the Mayor to keep his Sunday morning appointment with "Meet the Press." A crew was scheduled to arrive at his hotel in Dallas at 5 a.m., and although I had already prepped him for Tim Russert's experienced probing, the Mayor had decided he was too exhausted to go on.

"This is a national show that has promoted this interview all over the country," I wrote. "You're freaking me out."

I flagged Russert's producer, a native of Louisiana. "He's trying to bail, but I'm working it," I alerted her. Eventually, I prevailed over a very reluctant and weary Mayor.

"Hurricane Katrina, day 13. How goes the recovery? With us: the mayor of New Orleans, Ray Nagin. Mr. Mayor, good morning and welcome," Russert opened. "How about if both major political parties, Democrats and Republicans, pledge to have their conventions in 2008 in New Orleans?"

"I think that would be tremendous, you know, but right now, my sense is that there's such partisan bickering going on right now in the face of this awesome tragedy, that the likelihood of that happening, I'm not very optimistic," the Mayor replied.

I knew Tim Russert had done his homework and would most likely challenge the Mayor on some of his contradictory statements.

Next came the issue of the buses, for which the Mayor was prepared.

"We've all seen this photograph of these submerged school buses. Why did you not declare, order, a mandatory evacuation on Friday, when the president declared an emergency, and have utilized those buses to get people out?" Russert said.

"You know, Tim, that's one of the things that will be debated," the Mayor replied. "Sure, there were lots of buses out there. But guess what? You can't find drivers that would stay behind with a Category 5 hurricane, you know, pending down on New Orleans. We barely got enough drivers to move people on Sunday, or Saturday and Sunday, to move them to the Superdome, we barely had enough drivers for that."

"But, Mr. Mayor, if you read the city of New Orleans' comprehensive emergency plan," he said, "it says very clearly, 'Conduct of an actual evacuation will be the responsibility of the mayor of New Orleans. The city of New Orleans will utilize all available resources to quickly and safely evacuate threatened areas'," he probed before hitting hard. "Approximately 100,000 citizens of New Orleans do not have means of personal transportation. It was your responsibility. Where was the planning? Where was the preparation? Where was the execution?"

"The planning was always in getting people to higher ground, getting them to safety, that's what we meant by evacuation," the Mayor countered. "Get them to a higher ground and then depending upon our state and federal officials to move them out of harm's way after the storm has hit."

Like a Nascar driver shifting gears, Russert moved from buses to trains. "Amtrak said they offered to remove people from the city of New Orleans on Saturday night and that the city of New Orleans declined," he said.

"I don't know where that's coming from," the Mayor replied. "Amtrak never contacted me to make that offer. As a matter of fact, we checked the Amtrak lines for availability, and every available train was booked, as far as the report that I got, through September."

Finally, Russert brought it back to politics and asked about the performance of the President and Governor. I was hopeful the Mayor would use the opportunity to begin to build bridges with other government officials the city would greatly need as partners in the weeks and months ahead.

"Oh, I don't want to get into that, Tim," the Mayor answered. "I mean, I will tell you this: I think the President, for some reason, probably did not understand the full magnitude of this catastrophe on the front end. I think he was probably getting advice from some of his key advisers or some low-level folk that had been on the ground that this was serious, but not as serious as it ended up being. My interactions with the President is, anytime I talked with him and gave him what the real deal was and gave him the truth, he acted and he made things happen."

"How about the Governor?"

"Well, you know, I don't know about that one," the Mayor said.

Two steps forward, I thought, ten steps backward.

"We did not get a lot of other support for three or four days of pure hell on Earth," he continued. "There were resources that were sitting in other parishes. I just don't know. I mean, and then when a group did come down to review what was happening in New Orleans, it was a big media event. It was followed with cameras and with AP reporters, a little helicopter flyover, and then they had a press conference and it was gone. So I don't have much else to say about that."

"It sounds like you don't think the Governor has done a very good job," Russert concluded.

"I think there was an incredible breakdown of coordination, of resources, and decisions were made to move resources and to not move resources that just don't make sense to me," the Mayor said, now sounding dog-tired.

When the interview ended, I was so relieved.

The city was beginning to take steps toward recovery. In the Principal Federal Office housed along the Mississippi River, Admiral Allen's effective leadership guided an unprecedented level of mutual aid assistance pouring into the city. Across town, the city's new emergency center in the Hyatt morphed into a solid recovery arm.

Inside the emergency center, two uniformed soldiers appeared at my side one morning. Having observed me for a while, Major Mindy

Morgan said, "Listen, you can't survive with everyone pulling at you like this. You need help."

"What do you suggest?" I asked.

"You need a joint information bureau," she said matter of factly.

"Can you do it for me?" I asked.

"Yes," she said. From that day forward, under the tutelage of Major Morgan and Lieutenant Colonel Mike Pierson, aka Mork and Mindy, the 82nd Airborne assisted in the formation of a non-military joint information center to feed public information from local, state and federal levels to residents of destroyed communities.

I took Major Morgan in to meet the Mayor and told him about the help the military was providing. After she left, the Mayor called me over. "Who is she, Sally?" he asked. "Do you even know?"

"Yes, she's with the 82nd Airborne and is assigned to help us," I said. Certainly he was not going to start battling the Army, I assumed.

"I would be very careful about trusting these people," the Mayor cautioned.

"Mayor," I answered defensively, "we have so much information that needs to get out to the public and I am the only one here doing it."

If he only knew how desperate I was for the help.

As the weeks progressed and the Corps of Engineers closed the 17th Street and London Avenue levee breaches, a new storm named Hurricane Rita forced us into survival mode again. During this time, the Mayor wound up in a spat with Admiral Allen regarding when the city should repopulate. At the urging of Admiral Allen, I tried to get the Mayor to listen to his reasons for not wanting to let people in quite so soon, but the Mayor refused.

"They are in this together," he said.

"Who is?" I asked.

"The Governor and the Admiral," he replied.

It did not take long for the press to catch on as the Mayor began to refer to the Admiral as "the Federal Mayor of New Orleans."

John Roberts wrote, "Sally, Roberts at CBS here, how troubling is this pi**ing match with the feds over allowing people back in?"

When he was finally ready to patch things up, the Mayor presented an "I Love NO" T-shirt to Admiral Allen.

By the end of the second week, the Mayor had been granted time to reflect and sent me a heartfelt letter he had written by hand to the New Orleans Saints for their upcoming game. I tracked down the team in San Antonio and spoke to P.R. Director Greg Bensel.

"Greg, the Mayor wrote a letter to the Saints players. Can you talk to Coach Haslett and ask him to read it before the game?"

"Absolutely," he replied.

At work, my job title flew out of the window as I worked on the closing and reopening of public housing, a National Rifle Association lawsuit regarding our confiscation of guns during the storm and issues related to burying the unclaimed dead.

"How did I get the dead bodies?" I protested repeatedly to the Executive staff now back in the city.

I had also been acting as the Mayor's personal secretary. From Prince Charles and the King of Jordan to multiple French delegations, representatives from over 75 countries called to contribute to New Orleans, alongside over 80 percent of Americans. Political and business leaders, movie stars and humanitarians flooded our lines with offers to help. Overworked, I failed to properly acknowledge many acts of compassion on behalf of the city and felt horrible about the lack of attention given to the numerous people who did help or tried hard to do so.

Many African American leaders were outraged at the government's response, believing race was the reason for the delay. "This is Congressman Conyers' office," said a caller one day. "The Congressman really needs to speak to the Mayor because he is going to launch an investigation into how the White House botched this up."

Senator Barack Obama exhibited statesmanship when we met with him in Washington, but he indicated partisanship could be a major hindrance to the city's recovery. "Mayor, I'm here to help in any way, but it would be easier to get support for Louisiana if we could get Senator Landrieu and Senator Vitter to work together," he said. "Is there anything I can do to help facilitate that?"

President Bush took responsibility for the slow federal response to Katrina and the Governor followed suit, but soon political jockeying erupted again. The Governor, in an article in *The New York Times,* accused the federal government of "moving too slowly to recover the bodies of those killed by Hurricane Katrina."

It did not take long for the feds to fire back. "The state has always maintained direct control over the mortuary process following this tragedy," Admiral Allen said.

That same article highlighted deaths at hospitals in the storm's aftermath.

> A communications director for the city of New Orleans, Sally Forman, said today that all hospitals in the city have temporary morgues and that 'there are probably more bodies in those morgues.' Asked how it could take so long to recover the 45 bodies from the hospital, which remained there for more than a week after patients and staff had evacuated, she cited water in the building and referred questions about body recovery to the Federal Emergency Management Agency.

In Baton Rouge, Louisiana Attorney General Charles Foti would later file murder charges against the owners of a nursing home where dozens had drowned and then accuse a doctor and two nurses of administering lethal doses of morphine and Versed to four patients at Memorial Medical Center, an Uptown hospital inundated with ten feet of water. In New Orleans, District Attorney Eddie Jordan charged seven police officers with murder and attempted murder on the Danziger bridge, the incident that had left me feeling so relieved that we had finally gotten the bad guys.

With finger pointing in overdrive and anger over the failure of our federally-built levee system, any semblance of normalcy, like a sporting event, provided a reprieve from the devastation.

On Sunday, Coach Haslett gathered his team in the locker room and read the letter the Mayor had written earlier in the week. "Dear Saints Coaches and Player," he began, "I have personally witnessed firsthand babies dying, senior citizens laying down in the streets from total exhaustion and pleading to just let them die because they could not take the misery anymore," the Mayor wrote. "I have seen way too many dead bodies. I have seen and heard the heroes and sheroes who risked their lives."

Sheroes, I thought, this is a new one to me.

"Why am I telling you all of this? Because you are the New Orleans Saints," he wrote. "We need each of you to play hard every minute, every second just like our firemen and police did during their rescue mission. Even though they were dead tired, they pressed on. You must hit the field with the same determination that the survivors who stood on roofs and then endured four to five days in inhumane conditions in the Superdome and Convention Center until buses finally arrived.

"New Orleans Saints, this is your time, your season, your mission to lift the spirit of your fans when they need it most," he closed. "It's definitely time for the Saints to go marching into the Super Bowl. Let's do this!"

In a thrilling victory, the New Orleans Saints beat the Carolina Panthers 23-20.

Another storm hit less than five months after Katrina, in January 2006, when Mayor Nagin attended Martin Luther King Jr. activities traditionally held on the steps of City Hall. His talking points, written by Lesley then approved by me, were tucked in his pocket. He would later explain to me that he looked around and saw a number of politicians making dull political speeches, so he decided not to use them.

The Mayor wanted his words to be thought provoking, particularly to the displaced African American community. In a speech that initially confronted the black community for poorly raising their children, the Mayor concluded with bizarre declarations on life after Katrina.

"God is mad at America. He's sending hurricane after hurricane after hurricane." Then he added, "I don't care what people are saying Uptown or wherever they are. This city will be chocolate at the end of the day. This city will be a majority African American city. It's the way God wants it to be."

After the speech, the Mayor made matters worse with comments to an inquiring reporter. "Do you know how you make chocolate? You start with white milk and add cocoa and mix it up for a delicious drink," he said. "That is the chocolate I was talking about."

When I met him in his office early the following morning, apprehension filled his face. "What do you think?" he asked humbly.

"You have to apologize," I said.

Normally insistent about not appearing weak, the Mayor became more and more amenable to eating humble pie as we mapped out a strategy for damage control.

As we finished our meeting, Brenda walked into the Mayor's office, her calm demeanor now defiant. "You shouldn't apologize," she said. "Black people will not care about this."

But some black people did care.

Earlier on CNN, local African American civil rights attorney Tracie Washington said, "I am done trying to figure out what our Mayor is going to say off the cuff on any given day. It was an unfortunate goofball statement for him to make and all it has really done is make the city look just a little bit more ridiculous."

"Brenda, I've had calls from across the spectrum," I said sharply. "It offended people on many fronts." I began to add, "And what about whites and Hispanics and Asians and Indians who live here?" but I retreated. I had noticed that some of my African American colleagues more readily moved into a defensive stance when someone of stature from their race was accused of wrongdoing, often questioning if the person was being set up, if someone else could have committed the act or whether the circumstances were simply unfair treatment of blacks.

The Mayor spent the day apologizing, but I still received hundreds of e-mails from hurt residents of all races. "Sally," one wrote, "I have been proud to see you putting an optimistic spin on our mayor's occasional 'outspoken' remarks, but yesterday did a lot of damage and made me feel ashamed of our city. We are almost speechless."

"I am appalled at the Mayor's use of God in his words," wrote another.

On the scale at Winifred's house, I was 12 pounds lighter and still fighting nausea on a daily basis. Tired from trying to manage the enormous challenges, I juggled our move and family needs with work and a daily four hour commute. Our summer home in Mississippi had been hit by a 28-foot wave during Katrina and I hadn't even gotten there yet to assess the damage. Nearly everyone I spoke to had horrible tales of lost loved ones or an uncertain future, many bearing early signs of post traumatic stress disorder.

"The rabbit fell in the hole and hasn't yet hit the bottom," reporter Frank Donze said to me one day. I wondered how long it would be before we finally did.

The Mayor was also exhausted and expressed it in an e-mail to the editor of *The Times-Picayune*. "I am wearing down and having more days where I am not sure this is worth it," he wrote. "Not seeing much leadership and I do not believe the community understands the depths of our challenges."

I read that and wondered if the Mayor would resign.

To the contrary, he became re-energized by the challenge of 22 people who would qualify to unseat him as Mayor.

Katrina did not discriminate on the basis of race and neither did the rescuers. Our city was paralyzed with its command and control capabilities decimated, but Coast Guard, National Guard, Wildlife and Fisheries, military, law enforcement, FEMA and everyday citizens responded heroically to save Louisiana, Mississippi, Alabama and Texas citizens of every race and color from complete despair.

On the whole, Ray Nagin worked as hard as he could to fix the problems. For months after the storm, he placed himself squarely in front of grieving citizens at outreach forums and listened to their cries for help. But his hands-off approach to managing city government, combined with a nagging distrust of others, added to the stagnation prevalent in New Orleans in the years after the storm.

Positive signs do exist here that give hope to our community, such as safer levees, flourishing charter schools and, on a lighter note, the 2007 winning streak of the New Orleans Saints and their promising

2008 prospects. Volunteerism is everywhere and citizens have galvanized where government has failed.

On the other hand, Katrina cut a swath through our medical corridor, tourism sector and city infrastructure, while the murder rate has again begun to soar. Topping it off, slow moving and disjointed planning efforts have made New Orleans a case study in how to recklessly rebuild a major American city.

Partisan bickering, senseless bureaucracy and failures within government, including my own, may have delayed our recovery and stopped many from ever coming home. But did it kill the unique City of New Orleans?

No. Almost 300 years old, our city will survive.

Resting on its people.

Epilogue

After resigning my position at City Hall, I sent the Mayor a memo telling him that I had been proud of how he worked for the city after the storm. I'm still proud of the efforts of those who stayed to help.

Mayor Ray Nagin won a second term in 2006 and continues to serve as the local head of government.

Chief Compass resigned but would appear on "The Dr. Phil Show" to say Mayor Nagin, in fact, fired him.

Deputy Chief Warren Riley became Superintendent Riley upon Compass' resignation and now faces the daunting task of ridding the city of the unwelcome title of Murder Capital of the United States.

Colonel Ebbert still runs the Homeland Security office and still is pleased to be one of the few, the proud, the Marines.

Eagle Scout Marlon became deputy chief of police in charge of public integrity.

Greg the techie Meffert resigned from his post after creating the No. 1 municipal website in the country and has had several articles written about him in relation to a yacht he purchased (or didn't purchase).

Chief Parent still directs heroes and sheroes of the New Orleans Fire Department.

Chief Matthews left the emergency preparedness office and now works for the New Orleans Fire Department.

Doc Stephens still runs the city's Health Department, navigating the city through a crisis shortfall of doctors, nurses and psychiatric beds.

Dr. Juliette Saussy still serves as the head of emergency services and remains ready for the next crisis.

Dr. Brenda Hatfield is still the chief administrative officer for the city and continues to serve as the Mayor's most trusted ally.

Bodyguards Louis and Wondell are still bodyguards.

TD still works for the communications department and remains completely dedicated to the Mayor.

Audrey had her baby, a beautiful blond-haired boy named Tupelo.

Tami now lives in Houston with tens of thousands of evacuees.

Most of the executive staff members in this story are now gone including Sherry Landry, Don Hutchinson and Alberta Pate.

Governor Blanco is still hard at work, but decided not to seek re-election, which many historians believe is one of the best ways to protect her legacy of public service.

President Bush continues to be criticized for his flat-footed response to Katrina, despite approving over $110 billion in relief.

I hope Secretary Chertoff, in the words of General Honoré, secures some f'n successes.

Agent Jason Recher became the White House Senior Advance Officer and encourages people everywhere to help New Orleans rebuild.

Maggie Grant helped prepare the White House's "Lessons Learned" post-Katrina analysis.

Congressman Jefferson was indicted on multiple counts, including one that alleges $90,000 cash from a payoff was found in his freezer.

Since losing the mayoral election, Ron is back at the Audubon Zoo and Aquarium of the Americas and we continue to raise our family in the city we love.

Effects of Katrina

1,700	–	People who died
300,000	–	Homes destroyed
1.5 million	–	People who evacuated
220	–	Miles of levees "protect" south Louisiana
20' – 34'	–	Storm surge height above normal ocean levels
90,000	–	Square miles of land damaged (size of England)
95%	–	Oil shut down from the Gulf of Mexico
25,000	–	Businesses wiped out
100	–	Dead still unidentified in New Orleans
4,000	–	Pets that died
5,000	–	Fish dead at the Aquarium of the Americas
1.7 million	–	Electric customers without power after storm
120 million	–	Cubic yards of garbage collected
250,000	–	People still dispersed throughout the country
80,000	–	Homes still empty
$150 Billion	–	Estimated economic loss to New Orleans

** Approximate estimates

If I'd Have Known Then
What I Know Now...

1. Get trained! Read your government's emergency plan. Know the part you might play, along with the roles of other people and agencies.
2. Make a list of important items and understand your options in case of complete destruction. Know the types of problems produced by different types of disasters.
3. Establish contact with disaster magazines such as Recovery Times. Explore the use of the Homeland Security Information Network.
4. Purchase a small generator(s) and become aware of generator safety issues.
5. If your work requires communications, store batteries, a copier, a satellite phone, a wireless phone or Blackberry, a transistor radio, a flashlight, a whistle, a first aid kit, tools and a kit with personal items. Secure as many bullhorns as possible.
6. Explore the use of an Amber Alert or text message system during evacuations.
7. Consider laws or municipal codes/ordinances for price gouging, bankruptcy, garbage and debris removal and demolition.
8. Know the public information officers at all government and military branches including all health organizations.
9. Know the following terms:
    * National Response Plan, National Incident Management System (NIMS)
    * ESF (Emergency Support Functions) 1-15, DMort
    * Federal Coordinating Officer (FCO), Area Federal Office (AFO)
    * Unified Command, Office of Emergency Preparedness (OEP)
    * Emergency Operations Center (EOC)

- Joint Information Bureau / Joint Information Center (JIB or JIC)
- After-action report / Situation reports (SitReps)

10. Know the players in your Emergency Operations Center, the hub of disaster response and recovery.

11. Be prepared to communicate your needs in writing for transportation and fuel trucks, medical units, mortuary units, ice, water, power, etc. Coordination is key!

12. If disaster strikes, take notes for possible testimony.

13. Prepare a crisis communication proposal that can be submitted to FEMA immediately. Understand how a JIB/JIC works and start it immediately. Designate and create a media center. Make sure one person is assigned to media monitoring and analysis.

14. Immediately establish e-mail addresses on an outside server.

15. Set up a toll free number for an information tree. Include all basic services in your tree (i.e. Health/Safety, Housing, Business, Sanitation, Police/Fire/EMS, etc.) and update regularly. Look for a translator to prepare it in other pertinent languages.

16. Change all voice-mail recordings to provide members of the media with an e-mail address. Make a note to the foreign press that you cannot dial international numbers.

17. Create a repopulation plan and include an exit strategy for the military if they are called in.

18. Prepare a re-entry form for your citizens or employees. Be prepared to make copies and hand deliver these forms to as many locations as possible.

19. Prepare to put critical information online, on radio, billboards, flyers and digital road signs. Secure contacts now.

20. Establish a flow chart of all major challenges and include points of contact, key messages, and various agency responsibilities.

21. Accept all help and know that incident management team members will rotate out and be replaced with new people as you move from response to recovery.

22. Hold daily press conferences if possible.

23. Do not hold back critical information. Information voids can double a disaster. Take it from me.

Acknowledgements

I must first thank the people who rescued my family and me during Katrina. The tireless Winifred Ross and Kevin Reilly came through with a home and a spirit matched by few. Winifred opened her home to artists and friends alike, but she also took charge at the River Center in Baton Rouge, helping thousands of people get clothes and necessities they so desperately needed.

I must first recognize my teachers, from the early days with the nuns at St. Matthew, to the many along the way who pushed me to be my best: Mr. Murison, Dr. D., Dr. Day, Cornelia, Sally, Sam, Robert, Tim, Allen, Norman and Jay Alvaro.

I've worked with fine colleagues through the years, but essential city personnel (whom I shall not name but they know who they are), exhibited tremendous courage when we needed it most. Other people who weren't even residents, like David Kitty, Roger and Carey proved you don't have to live in the city to love it as your own.

Without Margaret Beer, Mark Romig, Mork and Mindy, John Crawford, Lauren Stover, Temple Black and the incident command teams inside the EOC, I'd still be treading water. Sgt. Dazet, Tom Atkin and many other experienced military personnel devoted themselves completely to Gulf Coast recovery.

Audrey Rodeman inspired the type of work, talent and professionalism that will keep any work truthful and its best. Leighton Steward's brilliance helped guide the notes and brain dump into a story. Jason Berry provided early publishing guidance, while Richard Deichmann helped later. Bruce Hoefer kept me out of trouble and James Nolan of the Loyola Writing Institute used his creative genius to turn a rough manuscript into a book.

Nothing in life matters without the joy and inspiration of my family, Ron, Cassidy, McClain, Dan, Catina, Jack, Ben, Mom, Peggy, Mary, Mickey, Bobby, Stan, Cindy, Susu, Granny, my in-laws, my adorable nieces and nephews, cousins and extended Gelpi, Counce, Legrand, Demarest, Forman, Burch, Thomas and Delph families and many of my friends, who often act as family, including DG sisters, forum, Friendship Group, the Queens and so many others who have graced me with their love. I must particularly tip my hat to Cricket and Critter, Guy Lanier, Havens, Parker, Megan, Helena and all of the girls and boys and their parents for tending to us when I was still in the city.

Finally, none of this could have happen if God hadn't answered my question: is this true, is this necessary and is this kind?

Printed in the United States
88181LV00005B/109-144/A

9 781434 329974